Praise for Taboo

As a woman, I know my entire existence is taboo - among men AND women - and at times, this existence is lonely. *Taboo* reminds me that no woman is by herself in this life. That there should not be any shame in sharing our experiences, from women's health and cultural/societal acceptance to the growth of wealth and sexual assault. Every single woman has a Taboo story. (bold this sentence) High praise for Taboo and the women that chose to share their stories, their lives, with the world in hopes to make our existence a little less taboo.

— Brandee Melcher, Award Winning Author, *The Break*

In a world where we often want to hide our stories in fear or shame, this fearless group of writers step into their truth in a powerful way. These stories are raw, poignant and courageous. You will be transformed and in awe of their daring willingness in vulnerability and honesty. Beautiful! Well done!

— Jessica Goldmuntz Stokes, Energy Healer and Award Winning Author, *Seeking Clarity in the Labyrinth: A Daughter's Journey Through Alzheimer's*

As young women, we are often conditioned to suppress our thoughts, emotions, fears, and expectations. *Taboo* invites readers on a transformative journey of self-exploration, uncovering hidden truths, and embracing the freedom found in transparency and authenticity. It serves as a powerful reminder and a much-needed permission to live boldly and unapologetically true to ourselves.

— LaNicia Duke, Author and Spiritual Life Coach

Taboo is a fearless manifesto that confronts the unspoken truths and societal taboos women encounter. With raw intimacy and empowering insights, it unites readers in the shared humanity of our experiences, reminding us of our universal connection. In breaking the silence around these forbidden topics, this book dares to challenge societal norms and invites us to embrace our authentic selves.

— Ashley Wize, Bestselling Author of *Motherland*

TABOO
Stories That Can't Be Told

Taboo
Stories That Can't Be Told

Red Thread Books

Red Thread Publishing LLC. 2024

Write to **info@redthreadbooks.com** if you are interested in publishing with Red Thread Publishing. Learn more about publications or foreign rights acquisitions of our catalog of books: www.redthreadbooks.com

This book compilation is initiated by Sierra Melcher, the founder of Red Thread Publishing. If you would like to be published as an author in our future book compilations such as this please visit www.redthreadbooks.com or email us at info@redthreadbooks.com.

Copyright © 2024 by Red Thread Books

All rights reserved.

No part of this book may be reproduced in any form or by any electronic or mechanical means, including information storage and retrieval systems, without written permission from the author, except for the use of brief quotations in a book review.

Paperback ISBN: 979-8-89294-020-7

Ebook ISBN: 979-8-89294-021-4

Cover Design: Red Thread Designs

The information and advice contained in this book are based upon the research and the personal and professional experiences of the authors. Some names and characteristics have been changed, some events have been compressed, and some dialogue has been recreated. Chapters reflect the authors' present recollections of experiences over time. The opinions herein are of each individual contributor. All writings are the property of individual contributors.

The publisher and authors are not responsible for any adverse effects or consequences resulting from the use of any of the suggestions, preparations, or procedures discussed in this book.

Dedication

To all the stories that died before they found freedom in the telling. To all the people who had to hold their truth too long.

Contents

Publisher's Note	xi
Foreword	xiii
Introduction	xv

CHAPTER ONE   1
The Power of Not Fitting In
By Roje Khalique

CHAPTER TWO   13
Soulful Wealth: Using Money to Heal and Empower Others
By Jess Bryan

CHAPTER THREE   25
Howling At The Moon: Harnessing Your Body's Wisdom to Thrive in Leadership and Life
By Bianka Kuhn-Thompson

CHAPTER FOUR   35
Bulbs & Butterflies – You, too, can transform.
By Rachel Macnaughtan

CHAPTER FIVE   47
Chasing Freedom
By Mimi Rich

CHAPTER SIX   59
Breaking the Silence: Confronting the Taboo of Sexual Assault
By Lesley Goth, PsyD

CHAPTER SEVEN   71
Pleasure After Pain: Ending the Legacy of Twisted Love
By Malissa Veroni-Prince

CHAPTER EIGHT   85
The Taboo Female Body: The Power of Our Cycles
By Sierra Melcher

CHAPTER NINE **97**
Carving Trails in Your Heart
By Kelly Upton Jameson

CHAPTER TEN **113**
What Will People Think?
By Anonymous

Thank you **119**
Acknowledgments **121**
Other Red Thread Books **123**
Red Thread Publishing **127**

Publisher's Note

Dear Reader,

Welcome to *Taboo*. We wish to offer a prelude regarding the sensitive topics that are explored within.

This anthology is a tapestry of personal narratives, each woven with authenticity and vulnerability. These stories include candid discussions about being human.

The stories in this anthology contain sensitive topics. They are *Taboo*. By definition, these topics can be triggering for some readers, and we advise discretion while reading.

At the same time, the intention of this work is to open space for healing dialogue and make more of the human experience acceptable to acknowledge. If given a voice, humanity's hard edges can bond and heal us. Silence serves no one.

We encourage you to approach these stories with an open heart and mind, knowing that each author's journey is a testament to the power of resilience, love, and the human spirit.

May it ripple,
  Red Thread Publishing

Foreword

Taboo: Stories That Can't Be Told is more than a collection of stories; it's a declaration—a refusal to allow silence to define us. Each story invites you to connect, reflect, and perhaps even see yourself in its pages.

These stories traverse the landscapes of womanhood, trauma, identity, survival, and resilience, shedding light on the shadows of the human experience. They candidly discuss what it means to be human in a world that often asks us to silence parts of ourselves.

The title, *Taboo*, reflects the essence of this work. A "taboo" is a social or cultural prohibition—subjects too uncomfortable, inconvenient, or stigmatized to openly discuss. These stories confront those forbidden truths head-on. By their nature, these topics can be triggering, and we encourage readers to approach the content with care and discretion.

Yet, the intention of this anthology is not to provoke discomfort for its own sake but to create space for healing dialogue and to make more of the human experience visible and acceptable to acknowledge. The hard edges of humanity—when given a voice—can bond us, heal us, and expand our understanding of ourselves and each other. Silence, by contrast, isolates and serves no one.

Thank you for joining us on this transformative exploration of what it means to be human, seen through the raw, unfiltered lens of women who have chosen to break the chains of silence. May these stories inspire and resonate with you as deeply as they have with us.

— Erika Shalene Hull, Managing Editor, Red Thread Publishing, Author, Expert Juggler of Chaos and Proud Primary Parent to Five

THIS ANTHOLOGY IS AN INVITATION: WHAT STORY WILL YOU SHARE?

Introduction

Welcome to *Taboo: Stories That Can't Be Told*, an anthology that dares to confront the silences we carry. Within these pages, you will find a powerful collection of narratives that shine a light on the forbidden, the unspoken, and the deeply human experiences that society often asks us to hide.

Each chapter in this anthology unearths a taboo—whether it's the pressure to conform, the silence around finances, the dismissal of menopause, the stigma of domestic abuse, or the shame tied to sexuality, menstruation, or mental health. These are stories of resilience, vulnerability, and empowerment that challenge societal norms and open the door to healing.

The authors within these pages have chosen to break the silence. They confront topics often deemed "off-limits" by culture, tradition, and societal expectation.

These stories challenge the idea that we must keep certain experiences hidden for fear of judgment, shame, or rejection. They argue for open dialogue, shared humanity, and the belief that vulnerability is a source of strength.

Reading this anthology may stir deep emotions. The taboos explored here can be challenging and, at times, triggering. Remember that every word represents the courage of someone who has chosen to step out of the shadows and into the light. At the same time honor yourself and read what you can when you can.

This book is not just a collection of stories; it is a collective call to end the silence. It is an invitation to see the world—and yourself—through a lens of greater understanding, compassion, and truth.

May these stories inspire, resonate, and empower you to confront the taboos in your own life and create a space for healing and dialogue.

— *Sierra Melcher,* Award-Winning Author & CEO of Red Thread Publishing

CHAPTER ONE
THE POWER OF NOT FITTING IN

BY ROJE KHALIQUE

THE GOLDEN GIRL – YOU ARE NOT GOOD ENOUGH

Growing up in East London during the turbulent 1980s, I found myself at the epicenter of rising racial tensions that gripped much of the UK. Our diverse community, with its significant immigrant population, became a flashpoint for the ugliest manifestations of racism and xenophobia. Several incidents are stark reminders of when I first became aware of the message, "You are not good enough."

At the tender age of 5, my daily walk to school became an exercise in fear. Gripping my mother's hand tightly as we crossed the zebra crossing on our way to school, I braced myself for the inevitable taunts. "Pakis go home," they would shout – not just children, but adults too. The memory of being spat at and our quiet resolve to keep walking is still seared into my mind.

On some Sundays, the British National Party (BNP) and the National Front supporters transformed our streets into a theatre of terror. I can still picture my father meticulously sealing and covering our letterbox before each march. I now understand the chilling reality behind his actions – the genuine threat of arson attacks, with fire sparklers, pushed through the letterboxes of immigrant families. The graffiti that frequently appeared on local street walls and shop fronts – "PAKIS GO HOME!" – served as a constant reminder of our precarious position in society – "You are not good enough." I've found it's not just racists - with their complete lack of humanity - who lump all South Asians together. I had teachers who shaped young minds and addressed me as Pakistani until one day, I asked, "Miss, heard of the Bengal Tiger?...." The response was, "Oh, I see" - she never considered South Asia's diverse nations.

As Christmas approached each year, I dreamed of playing Mary. But as I looked around at the few other brown girls in my class, I knew our chances were slim. Year after year, the result was the same. But brown girls like me were overlooked, our beauty and talent seemingly invisible to our teachers. I remember Charlotte vividly – my best friend with blonde hair and blue eyes that seemed to embody everything our teachers deemed 'beautiful.' Without fail, directors chose girls like Charlotte to play Mary, making them the princesses, the angels, and the center of attention. The roles allocated to me and the other girls of color were so insignificant. We were the silent shepherds, the nameless villagers, our presence more of an afterthought than an integral part of the story – the brown and the black girls were not 'pretty enough' – "We were not good enough."

I vividly remember white girls taunting me, claiming the reason for my waist-length hair was because my parents couldn't afford a haircut, their words laced with ignorance and prejudice. The memory of white boys yanking my long-braided hair, treating it as something alien and worthy of ridicule, still lingers. The very features that once marked brown and black girls as different, as somehow less than others, are now commodified. The hair extensions market, valued at approximately $5.8 billion in 2023, is a testament to this shift. The exact length and texture that once made brown girls a target of ridicule are now highly sought after.

This stark contrast serves as a poignant reminder of how deeply ingrained the undermining of ethnic minority beauty was in our society – the message "You are not good enough." Our features, our hairstyles, and our very essence were not just considered unattractive by others – they were often the focus of active hatred and used to emphasize our 'otherness.' The same skin tone that once marked us as targets for racism and discrimination has become a multibillion-dollar obsession. As of 2023, the global self-tanning products market is valued at over $1 billion. People pay premium prices to darken their skin, visit tanning salons or apply self-tanning products. The same shade that once made us "Not good enough" is now actively sought after, packaged, and sold as a symbol of beauty and status. This shift in perception is both validating and unsettling. The very essence of the hatred directed at brown and black people – our skin color and ethnic beauty rituals– has become a desirable attribute.

Looking back on the little girl gripping her mother's hand in fear or the child longingly wishing to be Mary in the nativity play, I'm filled with a complex mix of emotions. There's sadness for the innocence lost, anger at the injustices faced, and pride in our resilience. The message "You are not good enough" was never true—it reflected a society's narrow and harmful standards, not our worth.

Working Class – The Underdog

It was the first of many times I'd be reminded I didn't quite fit in. Little did I know, this was just the opening act in an extended performance of not belonging. As I grew older, the script would evolve, but the underlying message remained: "You are not good enough". I was born to working-class parents with immigrant grandparents. This background exposed me to classism from an early age. In a society that often equates worth and success with wealth, some saw my family's modest economic status as a limitation. I felt subtle and sometimes overt judgments about my intelligence, potential, and value based solely on my financial background. However, within my home, I learned the value of hard work, resilience, and the dignity of honest labor. This experience taught me to question societal worth measures and value character and resilience over financial and academic status.

I recall friends' shock when I got a 2:1 in my degree. These reactions were a stark reminder of the low expectations often placed on students from working-class families, immigrant backgrounds, or comprehensive schools. It was as if my very existence in these academic spaces was an anomaly, challenging the unspoken rules about who belongs in higher education and who doesn't.

My journey from a working-class background to academic achievement wasn't about proving anyone wrong but appreciating that limitations are often self-imposed or societally constructed. It was about understanding that success isn't always measured by grades or wealth but by the strength we find within ourselves to persevere despite our handicaps. As I look back on this journey, I realize that not having access to opportunities and resources taught me to persevere and to define success on my own terms. It showed me that true education goes beyond textbooks and classrooms – it's about learning to navigate the complexities of life with grace, determination, and an unwavering belief in one's worth.

Even in the world of business and entrepreneurship, deeper societal prejudices persist. The dismissive remarks I encounter from male friends — comments like "look at you," "keep your feet on the ground," or withholding congratulations until I meet an arbitrarily higher standard—are not mere casual observations. These subtle yet persistent jabs, often masquerading as friendly banter or well-meaning advice, undermine achievements and perpetuate a cycle of undervaluation. This dual assault on inherent worth (you are not worthy) and tangible achievements (your achievements are not worthy) creates a cycle of invalidation, with constantly shifting goalposts. Successes of marginalized groups face heightened scrutiny rather than celebration, reflecting entrenched societal biases. This systematic devaluation maintains power structures, forcing certain groups to continually prove their worth in ways privileged counterparts don't face.

Sexism – It's a Man's World

While learning to navigate a world that judged me for my skin color and my working-class background, I can recall my aunt's words, a chilling mantra that epitomized a twisted view of womanhood: "The best women amongst us are the ones that can put up with the worst man's abuse." This sentiment, far from being an isolated opinion, reflected the pervasive mindset that valued women based on their capacity to endure mistreatment and sacrifice. The culture I grew up in sometimes held a distorted image of what constituted a "good daughter, a good sister, a good wife, a good woman" otherwise, even amongst women – "You are not good enough."

Women are expected to mold themselves into silent martyrs, their worth measured by how much hardship they could endure without complaint and their ability to serve their men: father, brother, husband and son, often in the name of religion or culture. The tragedy of this situation is multi-layered. Some British Asian women were not only facing oppression from a male-dominated society but, in some cases, also contending with the internalized misogyny of their female elders, perpetuating the psychological and emotional wounds that pass from one generation of women to the next through inherited patterns of coping with adversity. A woman is deemed "not good enough" for confronting patriarchal systems, be that for having the courage to walk away from unhealthy relationships or even when choosing to marry someone of her own choice. Each of these actions, which should be seen as signs of strength, character and self-respect, instead becomes ammunition for ostracisation.

The struggles of divorced women and single mothers are particularly heartbreaking in all societies. Regardless of the circumstances leading to the divorce, women are often judged harshly and blamed for the collapse of their marriages—in some cases, even when friends and family are aware of their husband's extra-marital affairs. The stigma surrounding divorce is so pervasive in many South Asian Communities that even educated, independent women endure years of misery or even abuse due to the fear of bringing shame to their family or their fear of being seen as a failure by others, even when research shows a mother's self-esteem and mental well being directly shapes her children's sense of self-worth and emotional foundation. Even demanding basic respect and fidelity in marriage – rights – can be branded as combative – 'she's too aggressive' or 'she's too much' are often men's 'go to' descriptions. These labels are not just a dismissal; they are calculated tactics to silence and shame women who refuse to accept the emotional and psychological manipulation within relationships. Women are often trapped in a lose-lose situation: judged for being single, judged for choosing divorce, judged for their husband's extra-marital affairs, and judged for raising children alone. At every turn, women can find their self-worth being measured against impossible and often contradictory and patriarchal standards designed to control their freedom of choice.

Culturalism and Religionism

I was privileged to form friendships spanning racial, ethnic, religious, and socioeconomic lines. I vividly remember being called "too Westernized" or a "coconut" by Asian friends. These words stung not because I was ashamed of embracing Western culture but because they revealed rigid expectations about cultural authenticity.

Religious identity added another layer of complexity. I experienced how others could use religious identity to exclude, judge, or limit opportunities. I grew accustomed to judgments by all corners of my social network; "I didn't know you were a Muslim; you don't wear a hijab," "Why do you wear a sari? You're not a Hindu." "You're not English. Why do you dress like a white girl?" all of which revealed narrow views of religious and cultural identity.

This profound realization was both illuminating and emancipating: the complexity of my identity need not be simplified for others' comfort. It brought into sharp focus the sobering truth that I didn't wholly belong to any single group—not due to inadequacy, but because of my multifaceted experiences. Growing up amidst conflicting cultures and facing various forms of prejudice compelled me to question not my worth but the validity of these restrictive systems and values. I've come to appreciate the unique privilege of curating my identity, embracing elements that resonate while unapologetically rejecting those I deem unfair, limiting, or divisive.

Self-Worth Without Fitting In

Being an outsider has shaped my approach to life and helped me to experience and overcome the fear of judgment and failure. This awareness has been crucial in navigating societal expectations, particularly of womanhood. In a culture where a woman's value is often tied to her relationships with men, standing outside and challenging this norm or subtle and deep-rooted patriarchal systems can mean facing criticism. The cumulative effect of these prejudices is profound and far-reaching. It's not just about isolated incidents of discrimination or exclusion; it's the persistent, gnawing feeling that no matter how hard we try, we're always swimming against a current of societal bias.

However, not fitting in has been my most outstanding teacher. It has taught me to value my unique perspective and use my experiences to connect with others without borders. True strength can come not from conformity but from the courage to be oneself authentically, and our self-worth is not determined by how well we fit into outdated and prejudiced societal molds. Moreover, as people of color and from a working-class background, not having access to traditional opportunities compels us to dig deeper, find alternative paths to success, and charge ahead with no safety net. Through that, we can learn not to give up at the first hurdle but to embrace the fear of failure instead of running from it. This journey builds a resilience that allows us to get back up repeatedly until we hit the mark. Our struggles become our strengths, our differences become our advantages, and our outsider status becomes our unique perspective – sometimes giving us a 'unique sense of self and a higher sense of worth and even purpose.'

The unique ability to seamlessly navigate different cultural contexts allows us to see the beauty and value of various traditions and practices. This doesn't make us less authentic or less committed to any part of our heritage. Instead, it enriches our perspective and broadens our understanding of the world. We can appreciate all religions without feeling like traitors to our faith or background. However, this cultural fluidity often comes with its challenges. We may face pressure from both sides to "choose" or to be "more loyal" to one culture over another. We might be seen as "not Asian enough" by some and "not British enough" by others.

But these pressures miss the point of our rich identity, which means we do not fit in. In a world that often prizes conformity, our uniqueness can evoke discomfort in others—a reaction that speaks more to their fears, insecurities, and prejudices than our worth. This discomfort often stems from limited experiences and perspectives. The ability to think differently, connect across diverse groups, and persevere in the face of adversity become our greatest strength. Our multifaceted identities and experiences don't make us inadequate; instead, they equip us with invaluable skills—innovative thinking, broad empathy, and unwavering resilience. By not fitting in and through what others view as our failures and handicaps, we're not just surviving on the fringes but pioneering new ways of thinking, relating, and succeeding. This is the true power of the misfit, the outcast, the underdog – not just to overcome, but to transform adversity into advantage, turning the things that set us apart into the qualities that help us, and ultimately society, move forward.

The Freedom That Comes from Not Fitting In

For most of my life, I was baffled by how desperately people tried to put me in a box when I didn't fit neatly into any. I realized one can be many things simultaneously – Asian and Western, traditional and modern, rooted in heritage yet open to new ideas. This understanding allowed me to embrace all aspects of my identity without needing to choose or conform to others' expectations. I found myself in a unique position – able to bridge different worlds to understand and empathize with various perspectives.

Through my journey of not fitting in, in the relentless overt and covert message that "You're not good enough," facing challenges of always being the outsider looking in and finding the strength to hold onto aspects I believed in within my groups, I moved from feeling marginalized to seeing the power to be myself. Standing out leads to an inability or unwillingness to conform, which isn't a flaw but a conscious choice to challenge the status quo. As women of color who reject patriarchal-based injustice, we occupy a unique position at the intersection of different worlds, giving us the perspective to see the flaws in existing systems and the courage to envision and fight for something better.

Our willingness to reject unjust systems, challenge dehumanizing norms and advocate for all individuals' dignity sets us apart from those who are unaware and who accept or even perpetuate these injustices. This outsider status is not a burden but a badge of honor. It's a testament to a commitment to human rights and equality, even when it means going against the grain of society.

Living authentically means accepting that others may not like you, as it means sometimes standing apart from societal expectations. In worst-case scenarios, it may lead to abandonment, rejection and ostracization. However, it can also bring a profound sense of character, personal integrity and self-respect. In the long-term, authenticity allows us to form more profound, more meaningful connections with those who appreciate us for who we indeed are, rather than for an artificial persona we present just to fit in, just so we can belong, and to please others by hiding our true selves and striving to prove our worth via external validation.

Our encounters with intersecting forms of prejudice—from strangers and friends to loved ones alike- can deepen our empathy for others' struggles and fortify our resolve to stand unwavering in our convictions, even when doing so marks us as an outlier. In embracing this position, we can find purpose and not isolation. We can discover not rejection but the freedom to live authentically according to our values. Standing outside rigid boxes allows for connections others might miss, and this broader perspective can help us identify and transform outdated systems that no longer serve humanity. This is the power of embracing who we indeed are: it's the best of all worlds and bordered by none!

About the Author
Roje Khalique

Roje Khalique is a Clinical Consultant and the Founder of rkTherapy, a bespoke psychology practice based in London. With nearly 20 years of experience in mental health and clinical psychology, she has established herself as a pioneer in culturally attuned therapy.

Roje specializes in helping high-achieving women from minority ethnic groups in the legal, financial, and corporate sectors by providing evidence-based psychological interventions to overcome anxiety, overwhelm, and burnout. Her approach cultivates solid and healthy self-esteem, empowering clients to accelerate their career progression while achieving peace and contentment in their personal lives—without the need for self-sacrifice.

Her psychology services are offered virtually to clients across the UK, US, Middle East, Asia, and Europe and in person within London's exclusive corporate settings. Roje also provides intensive one-day and weekend therapy sessions. She developed the rkTherapy App Anxiet-

Ease: Therapy In Your Hands, which addresses mild to moderate anxiety conditions in six weeks through scientifically backed methods. Additionally, she offers online courses, weekly group coaching, and personalized one-to-one consultations to ensure comprehensive, fast, and easily accessible psychological therapy for her clients.

https://linktr.ee/rkhalique

Chapter Two
Soulful Wealth: Using Money to Heal and Empower Others

By Jess Bryan

What are the costs of grief?

The dogma of money taboos plagued my inner core, blocking all access to conversations about money, wealth and death. In this block, an oscillating thought process of lack, doubt and fear swirled between my goals and ambitions of prosperity and abundance. Breaking free from this, I discovered the inner alignment needed to propel my career down a very unexpected path while overcoming the most challenging tragedy of my life.

In becoming a voice, agent and coach for success in personal finance (especially when it's *VERY* personal), I struck gold in conversations that otherwise kept my clients and their families at war with each other and their inner critic. Maintaining the painful status quo of money taboo left my clients drained, feeling inadequate and hopeless in the pursuit of building soulful, authentic wealth. With my clients, we create "soulful wealth," abundance and prosperity that reverberate in all areas of life so much that wealth accumulation happens alongside joy and fulfillment. Together, we take on tough conversations, knowing the outcome is far greater than the sting of being uncomfortable with another person's words (or their own). The power they experience, when they align their communication with financial growth supersedes the never-ending blame, shame, and guilt that enters our relationships and bank accounts.

Soulful wealth involves taking on conversations that many of us hide from, pretend, and fake our way through. Soulful wealth is the antidote to lack, doubt and fear, birthed in the deepest layers of our being, where outside forces and voices constantly churn our desire for the synergy of money and happiness. Using the *energy* of money has lifted my clients from their tortuous silence, challenging society's rules of what it means to be wealthy and setting them on a path of optimistic creation toward their goals and aspirations.

Throughout this chapter, I implore you to step into *your* authentic version of soulful wealth—a type of wealth that leaves you feeling inspired, confident and connected to your declaration of life on your terms. You have the power to take on uncomfortable conversations, so I urge you to ask for authentic listening and then share your desires and *HOW* you want to achieve them. You are the creator and designer of your wealth!

As we explore this chapter together, you'll learn how to dispel the myths of money taboos that keep many of us constrained by pain, suffering, pretending, and failure. The brave, courageous voice that screams for purpose and fulfillment shatters the money taboo. Unfortunately, these myths often emerge at family gatherings, during intimate conversations with partners, or, even worse, after tragedy strikes.

Breaking the chains of societal pressures that weigh our money decisions involves audacious risk. Some of these risks led me to discover the energy of my soul that lay dormant, untapped, and guarded. In permitting myself to spend my money according to my desires, I transformed my relationship with money, my past, and the people in my life.

I'd always been afraid of the *force* of money conversations, especially with family. Amounts, big or small, both gave me anxiety. What I had known to be true about money had me stuck in an inherited mindset that became the foundation of my negative relationship with money.

The financial stigmas that consumed my family for generations left a trail of thorns for anyone who dared to tread the forbidden path. The familiar phrases would jump from one set of lips to another:

1. Don't let the neighbors know how much money we have; they'll take advantage of us
2. Asking someone how much they paid for something is rude
3. Never ask someone how much money they make
4. When someone gives you money, you owe them your life
5. If you work hard, you'll make lots of money
6. Discussing money should only happen privately behind closed doors
7. If you brag about your wealth, others will think you are too boastful and conceited
8. Rich people have an unfair advantage and get ahead because of inheritance, not hard work

Brushing money conversations under the rug was not just the norm but the expectation. In contrast, complaining, victimizing, and pretending were welcome sports in the world of "never have enough." These mental battles over money were passed down to me by generations of limiting beliefs and failed purpose. With a generous mix of cynicism and resignation, I became indifferent to the power of money as a tool for personal triumph over tragedy.

What many of my family members thought to be the best approaches to money left me with a poor financial literacy education, dozens of failed money management experiences, and ineffective communication skills. In other words, we couldn't be authentic with each other where we needed it the most.

I spent my teenage weekends hopping up and down I-95 with my godparents, Ted and Janet. Between frigid rinks and turnpike rest stops, they supported me through 12 years of ice hockey on AAA teams, then through NCAA hockey in college. Ted envisioned me getting a college education, advancing my skills, and learning to manage my money while standing on my own 2 feet. He was the most significant influence on my money decisions and was happy to call out the taboos that lurked in the shadows.

For Ted and Janet to pay the yearly hockey expenses, they needed to balance their retirement savings and investments. Although they were more affluent than the rest of the family, Ted knew this wealth was limited, especially as they were aging and paying doctor bills and copays more regularly. As college approached, Ted taught me what to expect for tuition, loans, and living expenses. Reflecting on these experiences and the paths I chose, I understand, more clearly than before, the impact of authentic money conversations. Ted and Janet helped me build a foundation of personal finance plus resilience to get through whatever life would throw at me.

Still, I fought my way through shoulds and shouldn'ts in my early 20s. As a working adult, I fell into the familiar financial challenges of my peers and was dismayed at the increasing responsibility of adulthood. Traveling, festivals, and happy hour were priorities that plugged away at my intended money goals.

During my travels and explorations, I observed the gradual evolution of my financial mindset, revealing the desire not to be indebted to my paychecks. Even more, I wanted to enjoy free time with friends, build myself up for my future family, and not worry about throwing down a couple hundred bucks for a flight. I knew I wanted to live on my terms; I just didn't know how to sit through uncomfortable conversations. I didn't know how to ask for it and make it happen.

Some of my internal conversations made me face-to-face with the reality of my decisions and mistakes, which cost me another level of financial comfort. As a young adult, I thought I had well-rounded money management skills. In life's pivots, I moved to another city to finally take one step toward the life I had imagined for myself. On a sunny afternoon in March of 2017, all this came to a grinding halt, demanding new resilience for something I'd never experienced before - grief.

This experience of death left me with a belief that losing a piece of my heart had no price tag. That death had no connection to money; we only suffered through it, hoping the pain would subside. Along with this belief, I decided there was no antidote for grief. I guess seeing my boyfriend's dead body and trying to revive any life in him with CPR scarred me so deeply I began to believe grief isn't something you can buy your way out of. Priceless grief caught up to me quickly, clouding my days with confusion, fear and torment.

In that first year, I fought the PTSD and grief with all my might, sometimes losing miserably. It hit at odd times, paralyzing my neurons and sending my body into convulsions with intense sobbing. The flashbacks of the paramedics, police and CSI team played out in the taunting rhetoric of sirens and shock mixed with intense stomach cramps. When the images showed up, I'd harden my battle stance, ready to take the blow, confident my gym stamina would help mop me off the floor. All the money in the world couldn't fix the past; it couldn't turn back time to reverse sudden death. But, with money, I decided to heal my soul while breaking the chains of taboo. I decided to island hop my way down the Adriatic coast to a 4-day music festival in Omiš, Croatia. By myself, on my terms.

In the impact of that decision, another familiar sensation crept into my mind - fear. After losing money on the apartment, psychologist sessions, a toxic relationship with a narcissist, and a chunk of uncompensated personal days, how will I manage to pay for this trip and come back replenished? How can I manage this trip to find what I'm looking for and not bankrupt myself simultaneously?

My money programming told me traveling was a luxury of the ultra-wealthy, a designation not listed for teachers. Traveling in Croatia for a month with a salary like mine usually meant seeking employment that would supplement the flight plus room and board. This dichotomy later became a driving force that propelled my success in designing a business and classroom that intentionally interrupts the programs and habits of ineffective communication around money.

The month-long trip took weeks to plan. Friends I'd invited said, "I don't have the time and money." Many didn't have the luxury of summers off or more than one week of vacation. A handful were bogged down by student loans, playing catch-up with their salaries. Many of us were still navigating the uncharted waters of a millennial career recovering from the recession. A trip to Europe wasn't on anyone's radar, at least not for the next decade.

"How much are you charging your credit card to pull this off? Do you really think it's a good idea for a girl to travel alone? Hostels aren't safe. Do you want to wait until you can afford hotels?" One after the other, I listened to suggestions on how to travel appropriately for a 32-year-old female. Between these conversations, I became more attuned to people's lack of financial planning. Many couldn't understand how to align their paycheck with their life desires and bring out the necessary conversations to ask for support to make it happen.

To break the chain of societal pressure, I overhauled my personal life, which was once inhabited by retail therapy and keeping up with the Joneses in exchange for opportunities to buy experiences versus things. To save for the trip, I intentionally shopped at second-hand stores, stopped buying new shoes and clothes for events, gave up caring what my purse looked like, accepted hand-me-down clothing from others and rented a room in an apartment with two roommates. None of this is rocket science for budgeting, but it involved giving up the societal taboos of how I *should* look, act, live, and spend. In becoming a minimalist hippy with a knack for music festivals, I discovered the meaning of "money well spent" in a new light. Throughout my experience of grief, my money mindset went through a metamorphosis that compassionately permitted me to do what I thought was necessary for myself, which meant spending my money in the most authentic way possible.

Croatia had always enchanted me, leaving me spellbound by the majestic blue waters, beaches and mountains. I thought that if I could find a way back to my soul, it would be via Croatia. I had been to Croatia twice before with Jim, so it felt appropriate to pull up to "Jimmy Bar" in Split to toast to a new chapter of healing from his death.

Sipping my coffee while waiting for the ferry to Hvar, I felt I had finally arrived, not to a destination but to accept the limitless *power* of money that creates life. I decided to listen to the inner voice that screamed at me to create my life with my rules, shedding the taboos, don'ts, can'ts, and shoulds. To do that, I needed to surrender my victimhood of money. I committed to letting go of materials and *things* that had no value or place in my life. I bravely challenged taboo by simultaneously taking on a healing retreat and financial responsibility.

Hotel travel reminded me of loneliness, isolation and individual pride. This trip allowed me to actively move away from those states that perpetuated my grief, which a hotel would only exacerbate. In my attempt to travel minimally on a cheap budget, hostels became a welcome agent for healing. My mornings were rich with sipping coffee with bunkmates, preparing meals in the kitchen, signing up for tours together and sharing stories of our lives and travels. I became friends with strangers, and in the process, I became friends with my grief.

Looking back on my decision to use the money to transform my energy and healing, I realize I crossed a threshold of taboo that propels my success with my clients and finances. Giving myself permission to spend my money on my terms without limiting beliefs and stigmas created the energy I needed to step into a new role as an entrepreneur. This energy has made all the difference in my relationships, business and client success stories.

Physical money brings pleasure, but the energy created by what money provides can supersede the material boundaries of pain, grief, and tragedy. Peeling through negative generational mindsets of money brings us to an authentic version of ourselves, creating opportunities to compound wealth. By aligning our desires while acknowledging our fears, we can use money to live happier lives, build stronger communities and reconcile the pain of the past.

How I bring authentic spending to business has diminished the force of taboo in the lives of my students and clients. As an 8th-grade teacher, I became a staunch advocate for personal finance curriculums in schools, so much so that I implemented a classroom economy simulation that helped my teen students experience real-world money decisions. Bringing the wisdom of my healing journey to my classroom, my students got to experience the energy of money through a series of decision-making scenarios that either boosted their happiness or sent them back to familiar taboos as a means of self-preservation.

Through student jobs, paychecks, hypothetical bills and spending scenarios, their relationship and mindset of money shifted to confidence, authenticity and power. They borrowed fake money, paid each other for job tasks, and became incentivized to use their money to make themselves *feel* good after an auction purchase they'd anticipated for weeks. In managing fake bank accounts and classroom responsibilities, they began to connect the dots to understand the force of money's energy in their lives. A force that gave them an eye-opening perspective of how their money decisions directly influence their happiness and fulfillment in life. Little by little, we worked together to learn the power of financial stability when tragedy strikes.

As we moved through each quarter, conversations erupted within our 8th-grade classroom and stretched into home life. Soon enough, my students' parents were emailing and calling to understand why their children were discussing emergency funds, fake insurance bills for a leaky roof, and the disappointment of splurging on an unnecessary bag of chips. Parents became allies to our classroom community, contributing what they could of their time and resources. Incorporating unexpected life events into a mock economy scenario completely transformed my relationship with my students, their parents and the classroom's energy. Money was no longer taboo in room 203.

In preparing my students for success, I intensely studied investing, spending, credit, debt, assets, liabilities, and retirement planning. Much of this was wisdom passed on by Ted and compounded by my enrollment in courses, seminars and financial licenses. From his deathbed, Ted saw the possibility of these endeavors and said, "You know, darling, don't be surprised if what you're doing with these kids turns into another opportunity." And he was right.

My search to heal my soul opened the doors to making such an impact in people's lives that they, too, have the power to disrupt toxic money mindsets and unfulfilling behaviors of money. By stepping bravely into my healing, I realized that my transformation is accessible to anyone willing to sit uncomfortably, declare what they genuinely want and take action.

Today, I help families build and maintain financial independence, which prepares them to overcome tragedy, loss and the unexpected while living an authentic life. In doing so, they experience the treasures of financial security and the freedom that comes with powerful conversations with authentic listening. My methodology focuses on personal finance education with explicit opportunities to take on conversations that put financial opportunities into action. From this action, my clients experience more intimate talks with their partners about money, rewarding conversations of retirement budgeting, and the relief of knowing that financial independence is one conversation away.

As CEO and Founder of my personal finance platform, **Future Empowered**, I continue to support families in identifying their goals, being critical about their spending, and speaking up to get what they want. In our "Wealthy Words for Women" community on Facebook, we share our most vulnerable moments with money. We inspire each other to break through the shoulds, can'ts, and don'ts. Money is no longer an obstacle but a force that feeds optimism. My clients actively pursue their dreams, take risks, and find solutions to fulfill their vision of happiness. Living an authentic life is truly priceless!

About the Author
Jess Bryan

Jess Bryan creates financial empowerment and action plans for families, focusing on women and teens. Through her education platform and company, **Future Empowered**, Jess is building a community of soulful wealth collaborations and working toward a vision of fulfillment and happiness for clients and partners. She is a voice and advocate for women's and teen's empowerment, working alongside them to support their growth, wealth and communication skills. Jess holds a Master's degree in Special Education and Educational Leadership and her financial license in life insurance and annuities.

Jess continues building her vision for ***Future Empowered*** by acquiring additional financial licenses and specialized courses on money management with effective communication skills. Jess lives in Miami with her husband and their cat, Jumanji. To learn more about Jess Bryan or find ways to work with her or someone from her team, visit https://linktr.ee/future_empowered.

Chapter Three
Howling At The Moon: Harnessing Your Body's Wisdom to Thrive in Leadership and Life

By Bianka Kuhn-Thompson

There's a whispered legend of 'the change' passed from mother to daughter, from age to youth. At some point, as a woman, you will float through a sheet of water by the light of the moon, and you will have passed through midlife. Age will come with wisdom, and you go on living.

Once we reach womanhood, the whispered legend changes. It's spoken woman to woman only in the dark of night, with hushed tones and coded words. The legend changes from a waterfall to a bare-footed journey over hot coals, lasting for years. This fire walk dries up our ovaries, shrivels our brains and turns us from a fertile and beautiful princess into the cackling, double-chinned mad cat lady smoking a pipe, face covered in spiky stubble, so the myth goes. Our intelligence and sanity will burn away, leaving us howling at the moon with a glint of madness.

Even if no one has told you *this* tale, if you have cultural roots in the West, you know this truth in your bones, womb and brain. You've read and heard variations of it, most, if not all, under the heading of 'Menopause.' Midlife for women is less defined by acquiring a new car and more by losing the car keys – and potentially your mind along with them.

No one warns us that menopause doesn't happen in isolation. It occurs in the midst of life when we should be getting on with other things, dealing with trauma, healing our bodies from cancer, or making a career jump. No one warns us that menopause weaves itself into the fabric of our lives, souls, thoughts, feelings, sexuality and bodies.

This all-inclusive, multi-faceted dynamic was how my wife, Fiona, experienced menopause. Fiona, I need to add, is badass. As much as life has tried to trip her up, she has danced through it. Fiona is a woman with stories to tell. Stories of overcoming mental ill-health and psychiatric diagnoses. Stories of miscarriage and postpartum depression, stories of illness and grief. Most importantly, stories of motherhood and cancer.

Yet Fiona is the most joyful, life-affirming person you will ever meet. Her enthusiasm is hard to match. She has parachuted from a plane, traveled, and learned belly and pole dancing. She will give indoor skydiving as much a chance as bungee jumping in New Zealand. Her struggles and stories of pain have instilled in her a zest for life that makes her grab every opportunity with fearlessness.

It's this inner strength and love of life with all its sticky creases and joyful sparkle that helped her – and us as a family – face her breast cancer diagnosis. Knowing it was detected early and had a good prognosis, we tackled it head-on, filling our life with talk of all things breasts. To our surprise, the world was ready to talk about both breasts and cancer. There was no shame, only treatment and looking to the future, as hormone-receptive cancer treatment included medically induced menopause that would deprive her body of all estrogen. Hormone replacement therapy (HRT) was, therefore, not an option, as the aim was to starve her body of estrogen to ensure the cancer didn't return. Like most women, we knew little about what that meant beyond tales of hot flashes, infertility and growing enough facial hair to qualify for an annual beard-braiding festival.

But what is Menopause? Clinically speaking, menopause is the process within the female body that causes the end of the menstrual cycle, extending over an indeterminable period and concluding twelve months after the last and final period. Yet what we often mean when we say 'menopause' is not the end but the process of menopausal transition

– or perimenopause. For ease, when I refer to 'menopause,' I mean both the menopausal transition and menopause. It's important to remember that every person assigned as female at birth will experience menopause. Women of menopausal age are by far the largest growing demographic group. By 2030, one billion women worldwide will have entered or be about to enter menopause. You either are or know someone who is experiencing menopausal symptoms, and most of us will spend about 40% of our lives in menopause. In the UK alone, menopause symptoms contribute to an estimated 14 million lost working days annually. Yet so many women (and men) know little about it.

This transition is so significant because it literally takes our entire body on a hormonal roller coaster. It's not just that our periods become irregular; our estrogen drops throughout this phase, having a knock-on effect on all other hormones. Put simply, the female brain runs on estrogen, and during menopause, the brain's estrogen tap is getting turned off.

If that wasn't enough, estrogen doesn't drop in a gentle and consistent downward trajectory. On the contrary, it fluctuates wildly, knocking our entire system out of sync, which can lead to a whole host of physical, mental and emotional symptoms – often all at once. Physical symptoms can include hot flashes, heart palpitations, digestive issues, joint pain, vaginal dryness, skin itching, an overactive bladder and even changes in body odor. If that sounds grim, it's not even an exhaustive list.

Additionally, menopause can have a considerable impact on our brains and mind. Think cognitive performance and memory issues, stress levels, headaches, difficulty concentrating and brain fog on top of sleeplessness. Lastly, there is the emotional fallout, which is often difficult to discuss. From fatigue, depression and anxiety to mood swings, anger, irritability and an intense feeling of overwhelm. Menopause, quite literally, turns your life and sense of self upside down. It takes you on a ride you feel you have no control over.

What's worse, in the Western world, menopause has been medicalized and vilified. The medical field has seen and treated it as a disease and illness, with extreme treatments that have included forceful removal of women's ovaries to being declared insane in the past decades. There was a belief that 'menopause was a clear prelude to depression and death.' For centuries, people have seen menopause through a male-dominated lens. The Western medical model has long favored men, often overlooking women's unique experiences and causing misdiagnosis when their symptoms differ. Instead of understanding the female experience of menopause as the natural result of massive transitional changes, we have ignorance, misinformation and outdated tropes such as the 'hysterical and emotional woman.' With the advent of unrelenting beauty standards, any transition in a woman's life comes with the expectation for women to spin it into a positive journey of self-discovery and inspiration. Want to know one of the most common outcomes of this perception that might affect you next time you go to the hospital? Women are less likely to have their pain taken seriously and, therefore, often given less pain relief than their male counterparts.

Alongside a mastectomy and radiotherapy, Fiona received medication to induce spontaneous menopause. From one day to the next, she had less estrogen than an 80-year-old woman. While on the surface, that might indicate that her body was able to evade the hormonal roller coaster I previously mentioned, it doesn't mean an escape from the tremendous impact of menopause. She just went over the cliff all at once, a bit like realizing mid-jump that you've forgotten you can't fly without a parachute as your body plunges downward. Overnight, this joyful, life-affirming, brave and optimistic woman turned into a sweating, cranky (think Hulk on a cocaine bender), forgetful and stressed person that she – and I – barely recognized. There was a pull between her fully embracing post-cancer life, learning pole dancing, modeling uni-boob clothing and singing loudly along to musical theater while being physically, emotionally and cognitively steamrollered by menopause. This impact was the one part no one prepared us for and where hardly any information was available. There were offers of conversations on breast reconstruction, side effects of cancer drugs, sex after cancer, how to talk to our child about death and cancer – but menopause and how to navigate it at home and work, think tumbleweed and polite smiles.

Considering menopause is a significant period of change in a woman's life, we expected to find as much information, guidance, and general knowledge as there is about the other two significant phases of change: puberty and pregnancy. Yet, instead of informational leaflets, we found adverts for incontinence pads and funeral plans for the over-50s women.

The lack of information and clarity created space in our minds for the myths and images at the start of this chapter. Whenever Fiona struggled with sleeplessness, I pictured her in a Victorian nightgown, wandering the corridors of an asylum, muttering to herself. When a hot flash irritably overcame her, I imagined a caricature of a hysterically screaming witch with hairy warts. None of which was helpful, and all of which was rooted in the patriarchal view that women lose their beauty, fertility and, frankly, the reason for existing during 'the change.' Fiona must have had those thoughts, too. She was looking in the mirror, recognizing neither the surgically altered body nor the emotionally and cognitively fraught woman staring back at her. The question 'What am I changing into?' surely crossed her mind, and culturally, none of the answers were appealing.

This standard of dismal information and resources was also apparent in the workplace. As a senior leader looking after a diverse team with wide-ranging needs, she faced high uncertainty at work. How do you lead a team when you are unsure of who you are, wonder if your mind will let you down mid-conversation, worry about spontaneous sweating, or just plainly don't feel like yourself anymore?

We all have a sense of self rooted in our experiences, abilities and environment. When our sense of self suddenly becomes removed, the natural consequence is that we question our abilities, capabilities and sense of purpose. Our symptoms' physical and emotional impact layer and feed off each other. All of this knocks our self-esteem, and we can't build it up without understanding various aspects of ourselves. Yet those aspects are undergoing mercurial changes and become unrecognizable in menopause.

As a Dramatherapist, a Systemic and Psychodynamic Leadership consultant, and a wife and partner, I was intrigued by Fiona's professional experience. When faced with big questions, we did what we always do: we got the books out—books on leadership, books on menopause, books on menopause in the workplace. None of them held the answers that we were looking for. The worst was the book that advised workplaces to give menopausal staff extra toilet breaks. It was a frustrating and disappointing process.

At this point, I'd love to write that I drew on my professional knowledge and skills, created an incredible 4 step approach that Fiona gratefully followed and that helped her re-discover her leadership edge, become "She-Ra - Master of the Menopause," and we all lived happily ever after. Let's be honest, though; who wants their spouse to be their fixer-upper?! That is not my role. My role is to imperfectly give her the space to live her experience and be there for her. My job is to remind her of her competence and offer her a dollop of love and understanding (alongside the occasional marital spat).

On a professional level, though, I realized just how taboo the conversation around menopause is for female leaders and organizations. For Fiona, it manifested in colleagues happily discussing the fallout from her cancer diagnosis but avoiding anything relating to her menopause symptoms. It manifested in the lack of resources, adjustments or general knowledge. She had to do the education and adjustments while navigating her changing body and mind.

As a female leader and drama therapist, this led me on a journey of discovery, and my mission is clear: to use my creative and systemic knowledge to help us thrive in our leadership positions while experiencing the various symptoms of menopause. First, we need to understand the biology behind menopause. Equally important is recognizing menopause as an adaptive stage we can control better than society and the medical field once led us to believe. Your brain is adapting – it's relearning how to function in your best interest without being fuelled by estrogen. Your body isn't working against you, however much it might feel that way. Your body is working, and it's working hard for you. If you only ever change one thing about how you think about menopause, make it this: assume everything your body does is its way of trying to support and help you in the only way it knows how.

Viewed through this lens, some of the symptoms, like headaches, hot flashes, or moments of anxiety, can, for example, be an early warning system that there is too much going on or that you need a break. Anger, for example, might be our BS detector, showing us that we have a lot less patience with time wasters. We can manage, influence, or even use other symptoms to our advantage, but this is only possible if we take the time to reflect on ourselves as a whole. Our sense of self, how we saw ourselves as leaders and professionals, what is changing, how we are different, and who and how we want to be once the turmoil has settled.

Assuming everything your body does is essentially its way of trying to support and help you is helpful in other aspects of managing menopause. It permits you to think about what your body now needs from you. It allows you to reflect on what it is trying to achieve and what you can do to help it achieve that. It might lead you to more rest, or it might lead you to say no to people or things. Give yourself permission to take a break, skip the neighborhood barbeque (or show up with a packet of bread rolls instead of a lavishly made potato salad), book yourself into a smash room, invest some time in coaching, do that dance class you always wanted to try – make space for yourself in your life.

As you read this, I can guarantee at least once you thought, 'Yes, but....' – I know because I have heard it from Fiona and said it at times, too. Take a moment to notice your 'yes, but.' This voice of fear is trying to keep us safe from perceived shame and embarrassment. It doesn't know that what it perceives as the safe zone is punishing and painful. It's saying, 'Yes, sounds great, but what if it all goes tits up (or tit up, in Fiona's case)? Stay in your lane, you might suffer, but you know how to deal with that. But you don't know how to deal with things feeling better. So just don't rock the boat.' – the voice will give you all sorts of reasons and excuses, from children to work commitments. I'm not saying there isn't tension in your life, and there aren't some non-negotiable priorities, but you should be one of them! There can absolutely be 15 minutes in your day that are just about you and finding your center of gravity again amidst the storms of menopause. If you don't know where to start prioritizing and finding time for yourself, head to my website, www.bravelyb.co.uk, where I share my favorite centering and cooling visualization with you and other tips and resources.

At some point, there might even be 60 minutes a month to discover a side to yourself you didn't know you had. Perhaps this is the time to challenge yourself to try something new that utterly opposes what you expect of yourself, whether open-water swimming as part of a monthly women's circle or joining a choir. Activities outside of family and work are especially powerful in helping you thrive as a professional leader. Any activity that pulls your focus away from home and work tasks helps our brain balance priorities more effectively; it's the power of play.

Just as with learning in childhood, play has a central role in helping us transition into the women and professional leaders within us. Play is any activity we do for the sheer enjoyment of doing it, and it speaks our brains and bodies' creative and accessible language. During those moments of play, light-heartedness and relaxation, we internally process our experiences and reflect. We only move forward if we reflect, and play enables that.

Some practical things need tackling. Too many women feel like they are in the early stages of dementia because their thoughts and memories turn into mercurial liquid before going up in smoke. There is a temptation to mask and hide the effects. Let me tell you right now – it doesn't work. It might help for a while, but it will cost you energy and anxiety. Yet if you start from the premise that your brain is trying to do its best for you, then perhaps you can help your brain by doing what works for it. I know from my work with female leaders that finding the right working system can make them feel like the queen of the organization and boss it on every level.

With all I have read, studied, taught and written, perhaps the most important lesson lies in Fiona's approach to life – embracing and maximizing every opportunity. Maybe by allowing ourselves to remain curious about ourselves and to belly dance, skydive, cocktail shake, moon howl, sea dive, marathon run or pillow fight, we can break the silence on this taboo one soulful tear, angry shout, joyful laugh, caring embrace and thoughtful conversation at a time.

About the Author
Bianka Kuhn-Thompson

Bianka is a Menopause Leadership Specialist, empowering female leaders to navigate menopause and thrive with renewed confidence and resilience through tailored creative strategies. Bianka holds a first-class Master's in Dramatherapy, a Postgraduate Certificate in Psychodynamic & Systemic Leadership Consultancy, and is a trained Four Seasons Behavioural Profiling Practitioner.

With over 15 years of experience, she brings passion and dedication to her practice, using humor and creativity to quickly get to the core of the issue. Her warm, empathetic, mission-driven approach ensures everyone she works with feels supported and inspired. Through her unique blend of Dramatherapy, training, and consultancy, she turns creative activities into concrete concepts, strategies, and professional development for individuals and teams.

https://linktr.ee/bravelyb

Chapter Four
Bulbs & Butterflies – You, too, can transform.

By Rachel Macnaughtan

I could feel the cold of the kitchen tiles seeping into my body. My four-year-old stood looking down at me with a puzzled look. Somewhere in the distance, the baby wailed. I tried to push up on my arms, but there was little strength. I lay there panting, trying to will strength into my body, trying desperately to find a way to get up and keep going. Eventually, I summoned enough strength to lift the baby into the highchair, only to collapse again. I tried to get my four-year-old to help me, but being on the autism spectrum, communication with him was often tricky. I do not remember if I ever fed the baby: my brain was so foggy, my muscles so limp. I felt like I was anesthetized.

Somewhere in the nightmare of that day, an acquaintance from my older children's school showed up, took one look at me, and rang my husband, ordering him home. My husband took me, barely conscious, to the doctor, and an ambulance rushed me to the hospital. The doctors could find nothing wrong with me beyond a slight increase in inflammatory markers. While waiting for my husband to come home, I had written a plea for help, which I hid in my clothing. When I showed this to a doctor, he called a psychiatrist to assess me and then a social worker became involved. After speaking with my husband on the phone, the psychiatrist warned me that if I did not leave my husband, I would be back in the hospital within two years. His reaction startled me and got me thinking in new directions.

We were a loving, happy, Christian family to the outer world. We both had degrees, respectable careers, a house, and a car. My husband had been an elder in the church, and everyone thought we were deeply in love. We had four beautiful children. So, what was happening to my body if the doctors could find nothing wrong? I knew things were far from well in our family and my marriage. On the surface, my husband was a dedicated and devoted husband who regularly sacrificed his career dreams and his health to care for a chronically sick wife. But, whenever I separated from my husband, my health would rapidly improve, and I would start to regain my self-confidence. After a couple of periods of separation, I began to deeply question the source of my ill health and why I felt magnetically drawn back to a relationship that made me so sick.

What I needed to transform in this situation was clarity.

Do you have the same need? Are you confused and unhappy with your life now but do not know what is wrong or what to do? By this time, we had been married for around eight years. I knew something was wrong with our relationship before we married, so why did I proceed with it? Why didn't I see the first warning signs?

The answer is surprisingly simple: my subconscious beliefs. There was perfect resonance between my inner, subconscious beliefs and what I was experiencing in my outer world. No one at that point had told me that **to change your outer world; you must first change your inner world**. Trying to change your outer world without changing your inner world does not work.

> To change your outer world, you must first change your inner world.

Many of us have grown up believing that our bodies and everything we see around us are solid matter. The particles that make up our bodies are vibrating. Every thought we think, every emotion we feel, and even the state of our cells have a measurable vibrational frequency.

The law of resonance states that we will attract people and experiences that vibrate at the same frequency as our thoughts, emotions, and cells. It took a long time for me to accept that my husband and I resonated perfectly. We shared many similar beliefs. We both believed the world was inherently an unsafe place from which we needed to protect ourselves. We both believed the husband was the head of the home. We were both harsh inner critics of ourselves. We thought we should not air 'dirty linen' in public. We both claimed to be Christians and to want to follow God, but deep down, neither of us trusted God. We both regularly experienced emotions like shame, guilt, and fear. Both of us equally wanted to escape these emotions. We both experienced similar health problems. However, in addition to the law of resonance, another universal law that initially seems contradictory, the law of balance or equilibrium, was actively impacting us.

In simple terms, the universe likes efficiency and does not like extremes. If you swing too far one way in one area of your life, the universe will bring in counterbalancing forces to balance out your extremes. The aim is to bring you back to a balanced, efficient center. You may wonder what this has to do with my relationship with my husband. I was incredibly empathetic. He was highly unempathetic and showed traits of covert/vulnerable narcissism. Our defense mechanisms also balanced each other out. He blamed and shamed me, and I usually accepted it all. He was resistant to change, and I endlessly tried to change and fix myself. He demanded, and I surrendered. Our extremes created an unhealthy form of balance. Any time we tried to lessen our extremes, it created an imbalance that would send us back to our extreme positions and behaviors.

So, our inner worlds were a perfect match. However, how we lived out those inner worlds were often at opposite ends of the spectrum. Add in childhood trauma, religion, four children, Autism, ADHD, and a plethora of health problems, and you have a complex situation.

Years in therapy helped me understand myself better, but while doing Peter Sage's Elite Mentorship Forum course, I learned that if we want our outer world to change, we must change our subconscious beliefs. After a year of experimenting, I devised a simple three-step process. The **first step** is to identify our current beliefs.

There are three ways to do this.

Method 1: Choose a method of recording: electronic or by hand in a journal. For the next week, note down each time strong emotions trigger you or you experience the feeling of solid resistance, harsh judgment, or strong attachment to something. You could be reacting to a person, a behavior, a thought, a dream for the future, or a decision. If you tune in, you will notice beliefs start to surface. Note those thoughts down. They are your subconscious beliefs surfacing.

Method 2: Set out to do something you want to do but feel strong resistance to. Note down the thoughts that surface as the emotions rise.

For example, when I first set out to author a book, I found colossal resistance rising. That is what procrastination is – resistance. As the emotional intensity increased, it felt like water rising in my body that would drown me. Then, the thoughts started to come. At first, I got caught up in listening to the thoughts. Then, I detached from the thoughts by thinking of them as a separate voice. The following is what I wrote down that day:

"See. I told you it would never work. You kidded yourself, thinking you had changed. You'll never be any good. You are in so much trouble now. So many others are offering what you're offering and doing it better. They work hard. You're so lazy. You'll never amount to anything. You've already failed, so there's no point in getting back up. You aren't even living what you preach. Just quit. There's no point. You've wasted so much money, and it hasn't even worked."

I will show you a way to change these beliefs later. For now, all you need to do is record them.

Method 3: Pick up almost any book on positivity or that gives you a positive thought for each day. Notice your thoughts as you read the positive thoughts. If your reaction is adverse, that shows that subconsciously, you believe something else, usually the opposite. Write it down.

Once we know what we believe, we can reverse it and develop a healthy, positive belief. So, **step two** is to flip the unhealthy belief into a healthy one.

Here are just six of the unhealthy beliefs that I have flipped:

My unhealthy belief: I do not deserve abundance.
Flipped healthy belief: *I am fully worthy of abundance.*

My unhealthy belief: Needs. What are those? Am I allowed to have them?
Flipped healthy belief: *I am assertive in meeting my own needs.*

My unhealthy belief: I am so hopeless and useless. I do not deserve to be loved.
Flipped healthy belief: *I am worthy and deserving of love.*

My unhealthy belief: I am such a failure. I will never be able to make my life work, and I've never been able to stick to what I commit to.
Flipped healthy belief: *I am committed to making my life work.*

My unhealthy belief: It is selfish to think I should get to choose my life. I should accept and be thankful for the things given to me.
Flipped healthy belief: *I take the initiative to create my life however I want.*

My unhealthy belief: Rights and personal power both sound selfish and entitled. Power makes people evil, doesn't it? I should just do what others tell me.
Flipped healthy belief: *I accept my Divine right to personal power.*

I am sure that I am not the only one. Often, we are quick to say we want a better life, but it is uncomfortable to look closely at what we have built our current life on. If you want to evaluate how healthy your beliefs are, look at your life and ask yourself the following questions. Do I have the freedom to construct my life how I want it? Am I able to be truly authentic? Do I have the health, the money, and the time to be all that I want to be, do all that I want to do, and create and contribute all that I want to? Do my relationships empower and liberate me, or constrain and restrict me? Do I have the freedom to be creative and express my originality? According to the dictionary, abundance simply means a large amount of something. It is the opposite of scarcity. In personal development groups, abundance refers to having the resources to be, do, and have more in life than we need just to survive.

After genuinely diving into my quest and journey, I have completely thrown out human-made religion, but I believe in God and that He is the source of infinite abundance. Under His guidance, I am reaching for a life of endless abundance, where there are no limits on who I can be, what I can do, and what I can have. You, like me, are fully worthy and deserving of abundance, love, and personal power. You might not believe that right now. That is perfectly okay. I did not for a long time either. These ideas might even frighten you. You do not need to be scared. Come with me. I am going to take you on a journey to a high place where I can show you a whole new land and I am going to teach you how to make it your own. The journey will start in this book, but I invite you to follow me beyond the pages of this book. Do not let the dark places on the way put you off.

To help you see this more clearly, take a moment to imagine that you are beside me. We are standing in an elevated, grassy area, and in the distance, we can see snow-capped mountains standing like sentinels against a backdrop of the sun and blue sky. We agreed to climb up the mountains, so we set off eagerly. We happily imagine ourselves climbing up and up to the mountains, but instead, we find ourselves at the edge of the grassy plateau. To our dismay, there lies between us and the glorious mountains, several deep valleys that do not look all inviting. As a matter of fact, they look incredibly dark and scary.

Now, back to my story. While I was in the hospital after the collapse, my mother came. After talking with the psychiatrist and social worker, we formed a plan for me and two of my children to go to stay with my parents. We told my husband it was so my parents could look after me in a quiet place. We started couple's counseling, and soon, I was back home and picking up life as if I had never left it. During my time away, I thought long and hard about ending the marriage and going out on my own. These thoughts were one of the deep valleys for me. The idea of taking on all the responsibilities of adult life and solo parenting was overwhelming. I did not think I could do it, so I returned to the life and marriage I knew.

WHAT WAS I MISSING? WHAT WOULD IT HAVE TAKEN FOR ME TO EMBRACE THE CHALLENGE?

The additional critical thing needed was a mentor or a guide.

Later, there was another abusive incident that would turn out to be a pivotal moment in my journey. I stared across the room at my husband, my heart pounding and my thoughts racing. I could not be hearing right. Did he just threaten to cut off all my finances if I did not shut my business down by the end of the day? As if he could read my mind, he replied, "Don't think I can't do it. I am dead serious." Part of me was trying to understand how my husband, who claimed to love me, could do that. Part of me was taking in the reality that he stood between me and the door with a steely *don't mess with me* look in his eyes. I glanced briefly at my handbag on the couch, which had car keys. I desperately hoped he could not read my thoughts because he was closer to the handbag than me. I was also considering the practical implications of shutting down my business.

Then, I decided to face those thoughts when I reached safety. Realizing I needed to move fast as my husband was still advancing, I hoped the door's deadbolt wasn't locked. I would have to get close to him to reach my handbag. Thankfully, the couch stood between me and him. My heart was pounding. Once I had made my decision, I moved fast. A minute later, I was out the door and running for the car. I drove a few streets away and pulled over, my whole body trembling like a leaf in a hurricane. I was terrified. I sat there for a long time, trying to work out what to do next. I finally found the courage to ring someone from church and, for the first time, talk to someone outside our marriage about my husband's behavior. *Airing our foul linen in public* was the hardest thing I had ever done. Hearing my listener's shocked reaction was precisely the sound I needed to hear at that moment to ignite my acknowledgment of what was happening. It surprised me and helped me realize that my experiences were not part of the usual difficulties of married life. It seems incredible to me now that I did not know that my husband's behavior was abusive, but I honestly did not. Sadly, I am not the only one. I did not like my husband's behavior, but I thought every husband behaved like this when they were in private.

The belief that every marriage takes challenging work was what I was always taught and reminded of. The lady I was speaking to was married, and I knew she and her husband had their issues, so her reaction was significant. For the first time, I questioned whether my experience exceeded everyday difficulties. You see, even in the earlier couple counseling, I had never dared speak up openly about what was happening in the home for fear of what my husband would do when we got home. I tried to use my eyes, body language, and subtle hints, but she did not catch on. It is unfair of me, but it has taken time to forgive that counselor for not noticing the clues I was dropping. I allowed my husband to gaslight me into agreeing to a version of the story where my collapse was because of severe allergies, multiple sclerosis, and, at worst, a nervous breakdown because of my weak constitution. This time, I began to question that story seriously.

Life continued, and there were enough ups to keep me in the relationship. Unbeknownst to my husband, just like the hidden growth of a bulb or the transformation of a butterfly, a gradual transformation was taking place inside me. There is no time in this short chapter to discuss all the mentors and guides God brought across my path. There was a social worker at church, our senior pastor who spoke out repeatedly about family violence from the pulpit, and a pastor who tracked with our family. Police officers, a magistrate, school leaders and family violence counselors also helped me. In the medical area, a naturopath and doctors guided me. My parents were a tremendous support, and there were numerous online and in-person coaches and authors. Each person pointed me to the next signpost on the journey through those deep, dark valleys to the mountains on the other side. There were also oases on the journey - periods of separation from my husband that became significant opportunities for me to catch my breath and develop new skills and knowledge.

These separations were critical in breaking the power of gaslighting and providing me with oases.

One form of abuse I have mentioned is gaslighting. If you have not heard this word, gaslighting is a form of emotional and psychological abuse used to disarm victims and cause them to question or doubt themselves - their sense of reality, memory, and capabilities. The abuse seriously damaged my self-esteem throughout the marriage. I doubted my intelligence, worth, and abilities and sometimes wondered if I was going crazy. During our separations, I discovered I was pretty intelligent, had an excellent memory, and was not going crazy.

One of my oases was when my husband was under an Intervention Order. This court order set restrictions on his proximity to and ability to communicate with us directly and indirectly. During that time, I had sessions with a family violence counselor who used Art Therapy with me. I still have a picture I drew during one of those sessions. It shows the soil line and, underneath the soil, a series of colored bulbs that I thought of as precious jewels. I treasured the bulbs because they represented areas of untapped potential in me, waiting for a safe and suitable time to burst forth and bloom. These sessions were a time to grieve lost potential and realize that my potential was not lost, just delayed – like bulbs underground waiting through an unusually long winter.

One of those bulbs was a hunger in me to communicate through writing. This chapter stands for that bulb starting to unfurl. You, too, have dormant, precious gem bulbs underground waiting to bloom. What I have written here cannot solve all your problems, but I hope hearing my story helps you on your journey.

As I write this, it is almost five years since I left my marriage for the last time. It took another two years for my husband to believe that I was not coming back and another year for the divorce and financial separation to go through the courts. I had little self-confidence and few adult life skills. However, away from my ex-husband and under God's loving guidance, many bulbs have poked through the ground and are at various stages of blossoming.

Another metaphor that I find helpful is that of a butterfly. As a child, I was lucky to grow up deep in the jungle of Papua New Guinea.

We had some beautiful butterflies. I still remember watching a butterfly one day unfurling its wings. I often wondered how a caterpillar could turn into such a different animal. Recently, I saw a video about what happens inside the chrysalis. The caterpillar dissolves into a chunky soup-like mixture and then reforms as a butterfly. It got me thinking of how I am slowly transforming by replacing my old beliefs with new ones, which is **step three**. I started out using a process called Psych-K. I have gone on to expand on Psych-K and take it in new directions. For over a year, I have quietly worked away at it. Every week, I upload three to four new healthy beliefs. For a long time, no one beyond my children seemed aware of any difference in me.

Psych-K is a process that allows us to upload new, healthier beliefs into our subconscious. Imagine that your subconscious is the size of an elephant, and your conscious is that of an ant. The ant rides on the back of the elephant. Guess who decides what actions you are going to take? When you feel resistance to doing or thinking something, that is your elephant saying "No." Psych-K allows the ant and the elephant to agree on a destination and connect the brain's right and left hemispheres. It has been amazing to see a whole new life of abundance unfold simply by changing my inner beliefs.

As I write this, I am sitting in the homestead of a remote cattle station in the Northern Territory of Australia. Every day, I go out with a personal guide. I have learned to fish, see crocodiles, go birdwatching, swim in croc-free waterholes, learn how cattle stations run in Australia, learn about animal conservation, star-gaze through a telescope, and so much more. Those things may not be your idea of abundance, but it is mine. Five years ago, I was confused, directionless, and possessed poor relational skills, not knowing who I was or what I needed. I had $20 in my bank account with children depending on me. I now have clarity, direction, exceptional guides, self-confidence, and a bulging emotional, mental, and relational skills toolkit. Like me and the bulbs and butterflies, you can grow and transform, too.

About the Author
Rachel Macnaughtan

Rachel is a teacher and mentor who uses a three-part process to help women adopt healthier beliefs and become fulfilled in their relationships.

Drawing on insights from her 20+ years in a painful and confusing marriage, Rachel helps women identify the unconscious beliefs that keep them stuck in unhappy relationships. She uses her teaching skills to map out a plan to replace these unhealthy beliefs with healthier beliefs.

Rachel is passionate about empowering women with the insights, knowledge, and skills to take charge of their ongoing transformational journey confidently. Before figuring out this process, Rachel struggled with disempowering relationships, depression, low self-confidence, and a long list of health problems. Rachel now lives a life of ever-increasing vitality, fun, freedom, adventure, and healthful relationships.

https://linktr.ee/rachelmacnaughtan

Chapter Five
Chasing Freedom
By Mimi Rich

Taboo is "an activity or behavior considered completely unacceptable or forbidden."
"A cultural or religious custom that does not allow people to do, use, or talk about a particular thing as people find it offensive or embarrassing."

— Oxford Learner's Thesaurus

I was born during World War II. My family's values were still steeped in turn-of-the-century attitudes.

To become free to be the woman I was born to be, my authentic Self, I had to confront many of society's taboos. As a result, my life became incredibly enriched beyond the bounds of society's restrictions and rigid rules. I have no regrets.

When I consider the taboos I grew up with, here is what comes to mind:

1. Restrictions on Freedom

What will the neighbors say?

In my family, there was deep concern for society's opinions. This was before social media, but in small-town West Virginia, everyone knew everyone else's business—and had an opinion about it! Growing up, I never remember being asked what I thought or felt about anything. I guess it was just assumed that I would go along with the program of what was socially acceptable.

Save yourself (translation - your virginity) for marriage.

The subtle message: sex is dirty, so save it for the one you love. This message made no sense to me. Of course, no one told me that sex was a beautiful vehicle for deep intimacy. Or that I should be very discerning about when and with whom I share this precious gift.

You will only be safe when you find a man to marry you and care for you.

So, marriage was the expected next step after college. In hindsight, I realize that really had been the prevailing wisdom for eons, particularly for me at a time when women barely had the vote, could not have their own bank accounts or credit cards, or could not lease property in their own names. An unmarried woman was often an object of pity, derision or suspicion.

When my first husband and I divorced, my mother literally said, "Oh, Mimi, I just won't rest until you find a man to take care of you." I was 33.

Travel Fiascos.

While young men and women today feel free to travel the world, in my youth, my family was very protective. Young ladies were watched over carefully. There were no opportunities to explore and experiment. My first solo travel was by train going to and from boarding school, a very circumscribed journey.

That protection without explanation did not prepare me for molestation. One Christmas vacation, on the night train from Washington to West Virginia, a young man in a military uniform sat beside me in the dark. Most passengers were sleeping. He proceeded to put his hand up my skirt. Raised to be nice and polite, I had no idea how to respond. I did not hit him or yell - I was paralyzed. Finally, I got up and went to the bathroom; when I returned, he was gone. I never told anyone.

On another Christmas vacation, the train from Baltimore ran late to Washington DC and I missed my connecting train to West Virginia. I was stuck overnight in DC with very little money. The train station was full of transient people and felt pretty unsafe. I got in a taxi and asked to be taken to the local YWCA, where I thought I might be able to afford a room for the night. The driver waited while I inquired and saw I was crestfallen and upset when I was told I couldn't afford a room.

Of course, the taboo would be something like "Don't trust strange men." This taxi driver said he would be working all night but that he would take me to his home where his wife would care for me and he would return for me in the morning and take me back to the train station. I believed him (trusted my intuition) and the night went just as he promised, with his kind wife treating me like her own child, feeding me and putting me to bed. My parents were frantic because I couldn't reach them to tell them what was happening, so they didn't know where I was all night. They were so grateful to the taxi driver and his wife that they exchanged Christmas cards with them for years after this incident.

I had wanderlust from my early teens. I somehow got the idea that I wanted to travel by myself to Estes Park in Colorado. (I had always heard the call of Nature and Mother Earth.) My Aunt Hester, my godmother, offered to finance this adventure. My parents surprisingly agreed. While they were so protective, it was strange that they made no effort to help me with the planning. I was probably 18 or 19. I flew to Denver and took a taxi to a hotel. I planned to rent a car to get to the park. But I discovered the next day that it was impossible without a credit card, which I did not own. After a day or two of confusion, frustration, and helplessness hiding out in the hotel, I booked a flight back home. I had no experience with creative thinking and problem-solving. And when I got home, no one asked how my adventure went; it was never discussed again!

Later in life, I ran away from my marriage to spend a winter sailing in the Bahamas. More on that later.

2. Sexual Freedom

Because of the Victorian attitudes of my family toward sexuality, I was given no instruction or support as a teenager for the raging hormones and intense longings my body was feeling. When I discovered masturbation at age 10, I was so excited that I naively tried to share this magic with my next-door neighbor. She looked at me like I was crazy. I wonder to this day what she thought or if she told anyone of my innocent discovery. Luckily, I didn't tell anyone else. My mother's attempt to inform me about my body and procreation was to give me a pamphlet to read with no discussion before or after. I read it and forgot it. When I got my period, I thought I was dying. At that time, menstruation was called "falling off the roof" or "The Curse!"

Three anecdotes from my mother's life offer some background. When I was ten and my sister was eight, Mother had an unplanned pregnancy at age 40 and was embarrassed to tell her mother. I guess she thought her mother expected her to be too old to be having sex with her husband. And she told my sister and me not to tell anyone; she didn't want us to say the word "pregnant."

When I was in elementary school and saw FUCK written on a school wall and asked my mother what it meant, she said, "It's two people naked together," with the implication that it was something dirty. There was no mention of the real purpose of sexuality or the beauty of that level of intimacy.

When I was a teenager, my mother freaked out when she found me reading "Lolita" (one of literature's greatest novels.)

So much of my subsequent history is directly related to the lack of knowledge and support I received about how to be a woman, to love my body, to honor myself and how to live an authentic life. Following my parents' advice, during my college years, I kept the eager, sex-starved fraternity boys at bay. However, during a summer internship in the office of a Republican Congressman in Washington, I was fortunate to meet an older man (Latino Cuba-American) who was an Administrative Assistant to another congressman. Hector was 30, married with children. He introduced me to the wonder of naked skin on skin and the delights of lunchtime oral sex. Gentle, kind, adoring: just the introduction I needed after my family's shaming and naysaying about the natural functions of the body. Somehow, it never occurred to me to save myself from him! I think the cultural difference helped circumvent the Puritanical life-denying attitudes I grew up with.

After college, I moved to New York City, thinking: if I can make it in the Big Apple, I can make it anywhere. In the mid-60s, I got a job as an Assistant Fashion Editor at Vogue Magazine, in the days of the editor Diana Vreeland - who really was a devil in Prada. And here's the next taboo. Through my work at Vogue, I met Gordon, a soulful, talented black photographer 30 years older than me. Again, another man outside my cultural upbringing who actually saw me and appreciated me for who I am. While we soared beneath the radar, our relationship as colleague, friend and lover spanned the next 40 years...and is one of my life's most significant gifts.

I married a wonderful, loving man, Laurance, who fit the perfect model for the husband I had been raised to want - Yale graduate, banker, and son of a respected doctor. Again, following the instructions for how a proper young woman behaved, I "saved myself for marriage" and was not fully intimate with him before we got married. What a sad situation to find, after all the anticipation and hoopla about intercourse, that we were not very compatible sexually, and I never felt satisfied with him.

I also realized that I had gotten married for the wrong reasons. Sadly, it was not because I had fallen madly in love. I married because all my friends were getting married, and I feared becoming an "old maid." But even more, getting married meant that I was no longer under the control and jurisdiction of my parents. However, rather than a step to freedom, becoming a wife was simply stepping into another set of expectations and obligations. Because I was not given any freedom as a single girl, I didn't know how to make considered choices and instead just found myself in another cage.

Just as I settled into conventional married life, the Sexual Revolution had begun, and my sexual longing grew - and again found a taboo outlet in three very different men. The boss at my subsequent computer job was Joseph, a Syrian Jewish immigrant with a family in Brooklyn; our lunchtime trysts brought me much joy.

And when my wanderlust finally found an outlet at a yoga camp on

Paradise Island in Nassau, the Bahamas, I also found a community of hippy sailors. In particular, I met two men, Richard and Manning, who seemed to see me, accepted and understood me. They allowed me to be exactly who I was without an agenda and helped me glimpse a free, adventurous life beyond the conventional. With them, I would spend a winter exploring the gorgeous Caribbean (when I "should" have been home in Vermont with my husband.)

I am so grateful that my husband let me have my wings, even though they eventually took me away from him. He somehow intuited my longing for freedom and was not threatened by it. And I am happy to say that my life is enriched by the dear friendship I continue to have with him and his current wife. While I respect those who can sustain a long-term marriage, it wasn't my path.

Later on, in 1983, I met the brilliant Chilean Buddhist neuroscientist Francisco. He co-founded the Mind & Life Institute, a think tank for scientific dialogues with the Dalai Lama from Santiago. I consider myself pretty smart, but I often didn't know what he talked about. In the '90s, he took me to a meeting of scientists in Boston, which included Mary Catherine Bateson, the daughter of Margaret Mead and Gregory Bateson, as they discussed, even then, their deep concern about the great extinction of so many species.

I never quite understood his attraction to me. But from the moment we met, there was an intimate connection, and again, I felt deeply seen and understood. When we parted, he said, "Remember that you are pure gold." It was hard to resist that level of appreciation.

3. Abortion

Having tried unsuccessfully to become pregnant with my husband for many years, I was beginning to think I could not conceive. So it was a complete surprise, in 1973, when I was newly back in Vermont from my winter of sailing the Caribbean, to find myself with child. Manning, the father, was an inveterate sailor. He lovingly said he would give up his ocean life and settle down to be a family with me. However, my heart told me it was not the right relationship or time to take on the responsibilities of parenthood. Abortion had recently become legal, and our mutual sailing friend Richard accompanied me to Planned Parenthood in New Haven, Connecticut, for an abortion and then to his mother's house, where they both cared for me until I recovered. While knowing it was the right decision, I was utterly grief-stricken.

The only other person I trusted to tell was my sister, who supported me wholeheartedly without judgment.

4. Spirituality

I was raised in a devout Episcopal Christian family. India called me early on when curiosity about other religions led me to write a high school paper about Mahatma Gandhi. My spiritual life also became taboo when I found more depth through the body awareness and meditation taught by my Hindu yoga teacher, Swami Vishnudevananda than I had found in weekly Sunday school and Episcopal church services with my parents. My mother interpreted my new interest in Eastern religion as a rejection of my family's upbringing when it was simply my interest in exploring other forms of spirituality. By the time I found my root guru, Tibetan Buddhist Chogyam Trungpa, Rinpoche, I had decided to live for two years at his Tibetan Buddhist meditation center in Vermont; my parents had finally settled into an understanding (if not a complete acceptance) that I was um...different.

5. "Illegitimate" Pregnancy

Another powerful taboo linked to sex was the family and societal horror of pregnancy outside marriage - my mother's worst fear. I think that is partially why I was sent to a girls' boarding school for high school. This was strongly connected to the "What will the neighbors think?" mindset.

So when I fell in love with Tom, a talented musician in Vermont, became pregnant with his child and moved into the beautiful, hand-crafted cabin he had built for me, they were stymied. We lived off the grid without electricity. We heated and cooked with wood, lit the house with kerosene lamps, hand-pumped our water, grew a huge vegetable garden and used a root cellar in summer and outdoors in winter for refrigeration. I am grateful for my parents' devotion to me that, despite their disapproval and lack of understanding about my choices, they came to visit. And when they met our beautiful newborn daughter, Sierra, the war was over.

While Tom and I never married, we successfully co-parented our daughter and continue to successfully co-grandparent our granddaughter Eden.

6. Home Birth/Beyond the Medical Establishment

Another taboo during that time was having a home birth. After meeting the cold, sterile attitude of the local male gynecologist, Tom and I decided that our child should be born at home, attended by a female midwife. I didn't tell my parents until after our daughter was born (fortunately healthy), knowing the pushback for such a decision would have been very difficult. In that situation, I again trusted my intuition and my woman's body, that it knew what to do as countless eons of women had done before me rather than the currently mandated standard hospital birth with the doctor in charge.

In Conclusion

As women, we have come a long way through the taboos I have described. And there is much to celebrate.

Thank goodness, we women (at least in the West) are no longer burned at the stake for honoring the moon's phases, using herbs and essential oils, practicing ancient healing techniques, midwifery, acupuncture, reflexology, astrology, and psychic wisdom.

Before 1970, women could not have credit cards, lease property in their name, be astronauts, attend military academies, receive paid maternity leave, adopt a baby as a single person, serve on juries or wear pants to school in many states. I celebrate that all that has changed.

We are no longer required to have a man to own property, bank account, or credit card; we go where we wish and love who we love.

We can revel in our pregnancies and breastfeed our babies in public.

We have a right to our bodies and decisions about childbirth (despite some male politicians who say otherwise.) We have the possibility and the right to bear children when we feel ready and not before.

When it comes to the law, we can be heard in courts of law as equals to men. Fortunately, I found strong support from a male judge and a female District Attorney when I petitioned the court to grant me freedom from an abusive partner (NOT my daughter's father) and to send him to prison for his vicious violence toward me. By the way, having freedom of choice sometimes means we should slow down in new relationships, listen for that wise, intuitive voice, note the red flags and be sure before we make a choice we might sorely regret!

The timing of my life has spanned the era from strict social convention to that of Free Love, Flower Children, Back to the Land and the idealistic Age of Aquarius dreams of a better world for all. During those years for me, I didn't have a conscious destination. I was somehow following an intuitive North Star, which led me to be myself, a free woman with a right to her own life. While I regret the hurt I may have caused those who expected different behavior from me, I cannot imagine making different choices. My path has always been mine to follow - and I honor that.

My North Star seems to have always been leading me to Pan-culturalism. From the kind but limited worldview I grew up with in West Virginia, I was drawn to *The Other*, the wisdom available to us from people not like me. Finally, I could never have imagined that the beautiful *Otherness* of South America would enrich my later years. Thanks to my daughter, I now begin to understand.

In hindsight, I see how I was attracted to perspectives beyond my roots and how much richness that curiosity has brought me. While I could not travel the world as young women can today, I found access to many other perspectives unavailable to those who stay home, afraid of the stranger, caught in the web of conventionality and societal expectation.

I wrote this chapter to offer some historical perspective. My wish is that my experiences toward freedom and in celebration of the Sacred Feminine will somehow heal the repressive wounding of the female spirit in my ancestral line and yours as well. May the Sacred Feminine take her rightful place as an equal partner with the Sacred Masculine as our world evolves out of the darkness of repressive patriarchy.

I hope that my story, ancient though it is, inspires anyone who hesitates to follow her dreams or is curtailed by fear or criticism from others.

Let go of all the old programming. Be yourself. Be the Light that you are. Be Love. You came here to find yourself, to have your unique journey. No one can tell you who or what that is - you must discover your light, beauty and wisdom by walking your path. The answers will manifest as you live that journey, step by step.

The End

Afterward for Reflection

Some pertinent thoughts from the incredible James Baldwin:

> "Pretend, for example, that you were born in Chicago and have never had the remotest desire to visit Hong Kong, which is only a name on a map for you; pretend that some convulsion, sometimes called accident, throws you into connection with a man or a woman who lives in Hong Kong and that you fall in love. Hong Kong will immediately cease to be a name and become the center of your life. And you may never know how many people live in Hong Kong. But you will know that one man or one woman lives there without whom you cannot live. And this is how our lives are changed, and this is how we are redeemed."

About the Author
Mimi Rich

Mimi Rich has been a Vogue Magazine Assistant Fashion Editor, a computer programmer and systems analyst, a waitress, a bookseller, and a yoga and meditation instructor. After earning a Master's degree in Counseling Psychology, she had a private psychotherapy practice for over 30 years and was Family Court Services Director at a California court. After retirement, she became an editor for Red Thread Publishing.

Currently living in Medellin, Colombia, she is a mother and grandmother, a lifelong seeker, a long-time student of Tibetan Buddhism, and a lover of poetry and music who holds great hopes for the coming generations to evolve the New Earth consciousness our beautiful planet needs.

Chapter Six
Breaking the Silence: Confronting the Taboo of Sexual Assault

By Lesley Goth, PsyD

Every 73 seconds, someone in the United States experiences sexual assault. This statistic sheds light on a pervasive issue often veiled in secrecy. I vividly remember the shame and internal turmoil I faced in coming to terms with my assaults, grappling with it for years before summoning the courage to speak up. The trauma I experienced, compounded by the stigma associated with my profession as a psychologist, kept me mute - highlighting the challenges even professionals encounter in addressing this delicate subject. Please be aware that the following chapter can be triggering if you have experienced sexual assault.

This chapter covers why sexual assault is so taboo and why discussing it can be challenging. Sexual assault does not discriminate based on age, race, gender, sexuality, economic status, or relationship status. Reporting sexual assault may intensify the feelings of shame and blame experienced by survivors, particularly when subjected to questioning or examinations by authorities that come across as victim-blaming. Experiencing this can significantly add to the trauma of seeking justice and support. Additionally, some survivors may encounter blame from their own families for the assaults they have endured. It's time for us to shatter the silence forced upon survivors!

This chapter also guides you through a healing journey by dispelling myths and addressing feelings of guilt and shame associated with sexual assault. We'll explore questions about fault, tackle triggers that affect relationships and intimacy, and discuss ways to cultivate safe connections for future healing. As an expert in trauma therapy for over two decades, authoring a book on surviving sexual assault titled "Unbroken: A Survivor's Journey After Sexual Assault," as well as being a sexual assault survivor myself, I draw from my personal and professional experiences to help you understand the journey of shame, self-blame, and healing firsthand.

It is perplexing that in a society inundated with sexual content, discussions about sexual assault are often met with unease and avoidance. This paradox prompts me to explore our cultural attitudes towards sexuality and violence. As Maya Angelou astutely remarked, "There is no greater agony than bearing an untold story inside you," succinctly capturing the profound impact of silence and shame surrounding incidents of sexual assault.

If you or someone close to you has gone through this, you know why it's such a sensitive issue. In my 20 years of being a psychologist and running a private practice specializing in all types of traumas, clients sometimes take ages to open up about their experiences with sexual assault. It took me months to share and understand the fears, shame, and self-blame that I carried ever since I was a very young child. Why? In my experience, despite having a safe space, my clients and I fear judgment, blame, and humiliation. We need to shatter this stigma so that it will stop being a taboo subject.

Let's look at why discussing sexual assault can be so taboo:

1. **Stigma and Shame:** I used to feel embarrassed or stigmatized, making it hard for me to share my assault experiences. Society's tendency to blame or doubt victims added to my feelings of shame.
2. **Fear of Reprisal:** I worried about retaliation from some of my abusers or negative repercussions if I spoke up. This fear

stopped me from coming forward and talking openly about what happened.
3. **Cultural Norms:** Some cultures view talking about sex or sexual violence as inappropriate, creating a barrier to open discussions about sexual assault and hindering efforts to support survivors.
4. **Lack of Understanding:** Misconceptions or a lack of awareness about the impact of sexual assault led to my discomfort and avoidance when discussing the issue.
5. **Legal and Social Consequences:** Bringing up sexual assault can have legal implications, such as reporting the crime or dealing with the justice system. Socially, it could harm reputations or relationships, discouraging individuals from speaking out.

Breaking the silence was the only way to lean into my healing process. My hope for discussing sexual assault is to continue raising awareness, supporting survivors, and fostering a culture of consent and respect.

Was It My Fault?

There are many questions that sexual assault survivors grapple with, making it a challenging subject to discuss. However, there is one question in particular that I have found to be the most common: "Was it my fault?" Before that, let's dig into what happens during a traumatic experience and how the brain typically reacts. Trauma essentially means losing all control, which triggers a deep fear of death. Your brain then kicks in with a fight, flight, freeze, or fawn response to keep you alive – a natural defense mechanism.

Our brain's wiring safeguards us at all costs and seeks clarity once the trauma passes. The brain craves closure and tries to regain control to prevent future harm. Closure, sadly, often means accepting blame just for the sake of having answers. However, deep down, you know it wasn't your fault, yet finding peace with this truth can be challenging.

The aftermath often starts with a flood of "what if" thoughts as your brain tries to restore security and control. Questions like "What if I had not worn that outfit?" "What if I didn't drink so much?" or "Why did my body react like that?" may lead to guilt and self-blame. These reactions happen instinctively during survival mode; whether you fought, fled, froze, or submitted – your brain prioritized survival above all else.

Don't be too hard on yourself regarding your response to your trauma. I understand that this is easier said than done. I recall a sleepover at my best friend's house in elementary school when her brother unexpectedly joined us in bed. He engaged in inappropriate behavior with both of us. This interaction left me feeling guilty, ashamed, and highly uncomfortable. Overwhelmed by distress, I called my dad to pick me up early. It was late, and I was eager to return home. Eventually, I confided in my dad about the incident, and he reassured me that what transpired was wholly inappropriate and not my fault.

Nevertheless, I found it challenging to avoid self-blame. I pondered whether I should have gone to my friend's house that night or if my feelings for her brother had somehow encouraged his actions. I felt paralyzed, so I allowed him to engage with me that way. I was distraught, convinced that the entire situation must have been my fault.

I eventually learned that my freeze response was what kept me safe. Also, over time, I learned how to squash all my "what if" questions that were torturing me. I started by swapping out my "what if" thoughts with "what is" or "what was." For example, switch "What if I had not gone to sleep over that night?" with "I went to have fun, but that does not permit anyone to cross my boundaries." This switch from "what if" to "what was" grounded me in the reality of what happened rather than getting stuck in self-blame.

Additionally, if you notice yourself freezing up instead of fighting back, recognize that your body did what it needed to do to survive without criticizing yourself. Recognizing your natural survival instincts can be empowering, rather than getting caught up in wishing you could have acted differently.

It's crucial to respect your body's natural responses during crises rather than blaming yourself for not reacting in a certain way afterward. Trusting these instincts is critical in navigating through trauma experiences beyond your control. Remember that each person's journey through trauma is unique – so embrace your body's protective instincts rather than criticizing yourself for ensuring your safety.

Triggers

Let's move on to triggers, learning how to understand them and navigate through them so as not to draw more shame into your healing process. In the realm of post-traumatic stress disorder (PTSD), a trigger is something that sets off intense emotional or physical reactions in people who have been through trauma. Triggers vary from person to person – they could be sights, sounds, smells, places, people, or situations that remind you of the traumatic event. When triggered, those with PTSD may feel extreme fear, anxiety, distress, and panic, along with physical symptoms like a racing heart, tight chest, or sweating. Healing involves recognizing triggers and finding ways to handle them.

Triggers can feel very distressing in the moment. One minute, you may feel fine, and then suddenly, you cannot see, speak coherently, or even stand up straight, as your whole body may react to a need for survival. Feeling triggered in a public setting can be embarrassing or humiliating. But again, it's so taboo to be able to express what you are feeling at the moment, as you may seem crazy or unstable. The irony is that the more you try to hide feeling triggered, the worse it feels.

Experiencing triggers is commonly a part of dealing with PTSD. For instance, one day, while I was out for a walk, enjoying music on my Sony Walkman, a man suddenly approached from behind, invaded my personal space, touched me inappropriately, and quickly ran away. I was initially taken aback and stood frozen in shock. However, as adrenaline surged through me, I sprinted home, called the police, and collapsed onto the floor. After that incident, I jumped at anyone approaching me from behind. Even when my son was younger and would unexpectedly enter my room after a nightmare, the surprise would startle me all over again, provoking an exaggerated reaction.

It's not just our minds that hang onto trauma; often, it gets stored in our very cells. So when something familiar, like a smell or sound, comes up, it can return you to that moment of fear and panic. Your body reacts as if that past danger is a current and real danger, all over again – like how I would jump at anyone who approached me from behind, even my child! The disconnect between mind and body can trigger that primal response of fight, flight, freeze, or fawn mode. Sadly, there is a lot of shame attached to feeling triggered.

When you're trying to manage triggers or reduce stress before they hit, it's common to resort to unhealthy coping strategies such as using substances, obsessing over food/exercise, or isolating yourself. But these tactics usually just end up making you feel even more ashamed, which is why people don't like discussing it. We tend to conceal our shame at all costs, though in reality, concealing shame can often push us into a downward spiral with no clear escape route.

Ultimately, the goal is to improve your ability to recognize, handle, and control your reactions when triggered rather than avoiding or ignoring them. Instead of resorting to harmful coping mechanisms, there are healthier alternatives that can help you manage intense emotions, connect to your genuine self, and feel safe in your own body.

Here are some of my favorite techniques that can help:

1. **Mindfulness and meditation:** Mindfulness and meditation can help you become more aware of your emotions and learn to observe them without judgment, helping you regulate them more effectively. My favorite meditation app is called *Insight Timer*. Over 35,000 free guided meditations are available to help you care for your mind and body when you feel intense emotions. Developing a daily practice changes brain chemistry and calms the entire nervous system. Try it for a few minutes a day for a week and see what you notice!
2. **Deep breathing exercises:** Deep breathing exercises can help calm your nervous system and reduce feelings of stress and anxiety. Here are two great breathing exercises you can try. I recommend doing deep breathing exercises daily.
    a. **Deep Breathing Technique:** Find a quiet and comfortable place to sit or lie down. Close your eyes and

take a deep breath through your nose, allowing your belly to expand as you fill your lungs with air. Hold your breath for a few seconds, then slowly exhale through your mouth, letting out all the air. Repeat this process for several minutes, focusing on the sensation of your breath entering and leaving your body.

    b. **4-7-8 Breathing Technique:** This technique involves inhaling for a count of 4, holding your breath for a count of 7, and exhaling for a count of 8. Start by exhaling completely, then inhale quietly through your nose for a count of 4. Hold your breath for a count of 7, then exhale slowly and completely through your mouth for a count of 8. Repeat this cycle for a few minutes, allowing yourself to relax and unwind with each breath.

3. **Physical exercise:** Regular exercise can help regulate your emotions by releasing endorphins, natural mood boosters. Even a short walk or quick workout can help improve your mood. If you're not a regular exerciser, try starting slow with a 5–10-minute walk daily. Try it for a week and see how it makes you feel.

4. **Journaling:** Writing down your thoughts and feelings can help you process and make sense of your emotions. Try writing about your experiences and how they make you feel. Have a notepad handy at work and home so you can easily express your feelings.

5. **Social support:** Talking to a friend, family member, or therapist can provide emotional support and help you process your feelings. Connecting with others can help you feel less alone in your emotions. Therapy is critical in this journey. Having a safe space to express your feelings without fear of judgment can help you heal and learn how to regulate your thoughts and feelings. Feeling secure, seen, and heard is imperative for your healing journey.

6. **Self-care activities:** Engaging in activities that you enjoy and that help you relax, such as taking a bath, reading a book, or listening to music, can help regulate your emotions

and improve your overall well-being. What is one small and doable thing you can do for yourself daily?

Everyone is different, so finding the best tools for you may take trial and error. It's essential to be patient and kind to yourself as you explore various strategies for regulating your emotions and managing your triggers. By incorporating these practices into your life, you can work towards feeling more balanced and at peace within yourself. The ultimate goal is to regain control and security within your body. Doing so creates more ease when navigating healthy relationships and setting healthy boundaries, which we will discuss next.

Boundaries

Enhancing your skills in setting boundaries is crucial to establishing healthy connections and genuine intimacy. I have observed in my life, as well as with many survivors of sexual assault, that it can be very challenging to set clear boundaries as we tend to prioritize others' needs over our own due to a fear of rejection or inadequacy. The habit of people-pleasing, often rooted in a deep-seated fear of abandonment and a belief that you are not good enough, leads to neglecting your well-being in favor of others.

Let's talk about why setting boundaries in relationships is super important:

1. **Respect Is Key:** Boundaries help us show respect for each other by clarifying what IS ok and what IS NOT. It's all about caring for each other's feelings and needs.
2. **Protect Your Feelings:** You're looking out for your emotional well-being by setting boundaries. It's like creating a shield to eliminate negativity that could ruin your happiness.
3. **Keep the Conversations Flowing:** Boundaries make communicating more manageable and more honest. When you lay down your boundaries, there's less chance of misunderstandings and arguments.

4. **Take Care of You:** Boundaries allow you to focus on yourself and your needs. They're like pausing to avoid getting overwhelmed and help you balance your personal life and relationships.
5. **Healthy Vibes Only:** When boundaries are in place, they build a strong foundation of trust, understanding, and compromise. You feel safe and secure, knowing you respect each other's needs.
6. **Keeps Toxicity at a Distance:** Establishing healthy and secure relationships is the primary objective. One aims to maintain a safe distance from individuals who exhibit toxicity, lack safety, or show disrespect. By doing so, one can effectively prevent triggering trauma responses when engaging with others.
7. **Eliminates People Pleasing:** To overcome people-pleasing tendencies and set boundaries effectively, you must learn to handle the discomfort of upsetting others. The goal is to remember that each individual is responsible for their own emotions and reactions – don't bear the burden of ensuring everyone else is happy at the cost of your well-being. It's not worth sacrificing for people who do not truly value and appreciate you.

So, boundaries are the secret sauce to keeping your relationships healthy and positive. Healthy boundaries promote respect, communication, emotional well-being, and self-care, keeping things running smoothly. However, sometimes boundaries are disregarded. I went on a first date where I explicitly mentioned at the end of the evening that there would be no intimacy. Although I had been drinking, I believed I communicated my intentions clearly—that my date could drive me home and nothing more would happen. However, that did not prevent this person from coming inside, which led to a sequence of events where one thing escalated into another because he completely disregarded my boundaries. I felt shocked, stunned, ashamed, and devastated. I genuinely liked him, but he failed to respect my limits!

So that you know, those who genuinely care about you will always respect your boundaries. You shouldn't have to struggle to make them acknowledge and honor your comfort areas. How individuals react to your boundaries can give you a clear picture of who you can trust. It's an excellent way to set firmer boundaries with those who aren't safe but with whom you still want to connect. With trustworthy people, you can have more flexible boundaries for closer interaction.

In this chapter, we've been diving into why sexual assault is such a taboo topic in our society and how feelings of shame, guilt, and self-blame can hinder survivors from healing openly and honestly. By shifting from 'what if' scenarios to 'what is,' pinpointing your triggers, and starting to establish healthy boundaries for your safety and well-being, you're taking steps to break the stigma and shame survivors often carry. Always remember, you possess the incredible power to heal, thrive, and mend the fragments of yourself that once seemed broken, forging the life you undeniably deserve.

About the Author
Lesley Goth

Lesley Goth is a licensed clinical psychologist with over 20 years of experience in private practice, dedicated to supporting individuals on their journey to healing. As an author and speaker, Lesley is passionate about sharing knowledge and insights that empower others, particularly those who have experienced trauma. Her work primarily focuses on helping sexual assault survivors navigate the complexities of their healing journey, utilizing Eye Movement Desensitization and Reprocessing (EMDR) therapy as a transformative tool for recovery.

Through Lesley's practice, writing, and speaking, she strives to create a safe and compassionate space where clients can explore their experiences, reclaim their narratives, and foster resilience. Lesley believes in the profound healing capacity within each person and is committed to guiding them toward a brighter, more hopeful future.

To get Lesley's free resource, *Healing Foundations: A Resource to Start Healing After Sexual Assault*, or to find ways to work with her or someone from her team, go to https://linktr.ee/lesleygoth for more information.

Chapter Seven
Pleasure After Pain: Ending the Legacy of Twisted Love

By Malissa Veroni-Prince

I didn't know I could say no. I didn't even know I had the option. The pain hit me like a thousand tiny cuts, slicing me open from the inside out. The weight of his body crushed me, trapping me beneath him as if I were nothing more than a lifeless rag. His thick, girthy penis forced its way inside me, tearing through my delicate flesh, ripping me apart as if being stabbed with a jagged, rusted old blade. The burning pain in my vulva radiated through my entire body, sending shock waves of agony that left me trembling, still, and with every nerve screaming in quiet protest. I was frozen, paralyzed by fear, but I moved —I don't know what I was doing. I didn't know what was happening. That's what I was supposed to do, right? Move. Make him happy. Make him love me. After all, I'm a people pleaser, and he looks like he likes it.

I was desperate for someone to like me, someone to love me, even if it meant enduring this—this horror, this violation. This person took what wasn't his to take, and I let him. Because what else was I supposed to do? It wasn't "real rape," after all. It was my first time, and he said he was my boyfriend. So, I convinced myself it was okay. I was safe, wasn't I? After all, it happened in my mom's car, the one I borrowed to drive to choir practice that night. I used to sing like an angel. My voice was a beacon of light, reaching the heavens with a range that could bring anyone to tears. But that night, there was no music, angelic chorus, or divine harmony. There were tears alongside the brutal, violent silence of my shattered innocence, a longing to be truly loved, accepted, and seen for me. "I'm a good girl."

It happened in the parking lot of a church. I told myself I was protected because God loves me—He loves everyone, right? But while I was singing in the choir earlier, hitting every note with precision, nothing like that happened in Mom's car. My silent screams were swallowed by the darkness, echoing back at me as if the very walls of the church were mocking my pain. While I don't want to name the church or the other person, I found it symbolic that it had "Mother" in the church's name.

Why, you may ask?

I got pregnant. That's not supposed to happen, right? Someone told me that during rape, the trauma would protect me from pregnancy. That's God's way of shielding us, they said. In its infinite wisdom, the body knows to shut down to prevent the seed of violence from taking root. But there I was, a child of God now unknowingly carrying a child. Another person said to me that if I touched a boy—even my father or brother—I could get pregnant. So what was it? How did this happen? I was an easy target—naive, trusting, eager to be loved and please others.

I blamed my mother for this.

She trained me for this.

I also slightly blamed my strict religious upbringing that promoted my "pureness," naivete, and, to be honest, "for being set up that way."

I didn't place all the blame on the man who raped me. It wasn't some Freudian deflection where everything becomes pinned on the mother. It simply felt easier, at the time, to focus my pain on those who should have protected me—the ones who began the cycle of betrayal. Both my 'boyfriend' and my 'mother' violated me in their unique ways, and that hurt ran deep.

The surgeries that came after, the endless medical treatments, the lingering health issues, and the haunting nightmares only solidified my belief that it was all my fault, and, all the while, I was instructed to pray for my unborn child and stay silent about what had happened. 'People will look down on you,' they warned. 'Don't let them see your shameful sin.'

But it wasn't the sexual assault or the survival tactics that truly traumatized me.

What really fucked me up was being 'loved' by a narcissistic parent, then spending my life chasing love in all the wrong places. Honestly, I didn't even know what I was dealing with—most of us don't. With a narcissistic parent, love felt like a trap. Validation came with strings attached. And I was taught that pain was just part of being loved.

The real trauma came from years of living under that shadow—the constant confusion, crippling self-doubt, and the endless search for approval that never came. It came from the relationships I pursued, trying to fill the void left by that early, twisted version of 'love.' And it came from not knowing any better, believing this was normal—never stopping to question whether things could, or should, be any different.

Growing up with a narcissistic parent, dating someone with similar traits, and later working for them caused more pain than any physical injury I endured as a young woman that fateful night in my mother's car. Narcissists surrounded me my whole life. I didn't recognize the pattern until much later. I thought I was crazy.

I was overwhelmingly confused while grappling with everyone else's 'craziness' and believing it was all my fault. Despite the blurry patterns, the symptoms of my upbringing were crystal clear: constant confusion, crippling self-doubt, and never feeling good enough were at my core. I was always trying to improve, but I never wanted to intrude on anyone or anything. The inexplicable symptoms that made me seem 'crazy' to both others and the medical system baffled us all. Sleepless nights, exhausted days, and constant unease became my norm. And then there was my so-called 'superpower'—a curse—of trying to predict my own and others' next moves, often incorrectly—a nightmare no one would choose. The nightmares I had while sleeping felt like a welcome break compared to living them.

Fast forward a year, and I sat in a university class on human sexuality. That's when I learned that what I had experienced wasn't sex—it was abuse. The more I learned, the deeper the rabbit hole went, plunging me into breakdowns, mental health crises, and a world of bullshit that I never knew existed (or wanted to know existed).

I questioned everything—including myself.

People say God helps those who help themselves. But how can we help ourselves when no one teaches us how? They discourage us from forming opinions or expressing our wants and needs. Narcissists raise us, claim to love us, and we love them back, often to our detriment. We try to fix them instead of focusing on our healing. I often wondered why God gave me my particular mother. Why did God allow that man, and later men, to hurt me? Why did God permit so much pain for me and others?

The pain was too much, and I was determined to find out why. I longed to become a social worker and knew I needed to 'deal with my shit' first before I could serve others effectively. So, I chose the uncertain path of healing, driven by the belief that we all deserve better than the suffering life has thrown us.

After more than a decade of helping others (and myself) heal from narcissistic abuse and sexual trauma, I've come to realize that one of the most crucial steps in recovery is rediscovering who you are, redefining joy, and learning to embrace it. Supporting extraordinary individuals navigating their healing journeys through similar darkness is an absolute privilege. I hold this with great responsibility and do not take it lightly.

Let me share a story that illustrates this process. One of the remarkable clients I serve, whom I'll call Sarah, came to me with a story that echoed parts of my past. While Sarah thankfully didn't experience the same sexual assault I did, she faced what I describe as "psychological rape." It is just as ruinous and life-changing.

Sarah's journey, though uniquely her own, echoed a shared thread of deep emotional pain that closely mirrored mine. She came to see me with concerns about memory loss, depression, anxiety, and fearing she might be developing dementia. Through our work together, we discovered that her symptoms were not due to "bad water" or burnout from her healthcare job during the pandemic. Instead, they were rooted in toxic relationships—with a controlling mother and a once-charming partner. Unknowingly entangled in narcissistic abuse, Sarah's body had sensed the problem long before she could articulate it.

Her struggle with covert control, gaslighting, and emotional turbulence was overwhelming. It took immense courage for Sarah to confront these hidden and damaging dynamics, and I deeply admire her bravery.

Who is Sarah? Who are we? We are individuals raised by narcissists who mistook their abuse for love and attention. But where does this leave us? Are we destined to feel hopeless and alone, trapped in a cycle of dysfunction that haunts us and others?

No!

But let's face it and be honest here... NO ONE EVER signs up for this type of abuse, maltreatment, and misery. NO ONE!

Reflecting on Sarah's journey (as well as my own), I've come to understand that my work extends beyond addressing the trauma inflicted by others. It's also about helping people heal from the self-inflicted wounds that arise from seeking love and validation. Like Sarah, we are individuals raised by narcissists, mistaking their abuse for love and attention. But this does not mean our destiny is to remain trapped in a cycle of dysfunction and hopelessness.

Like all my clients, Sarah is a true warrior—lovely, passionate, and hardworking. Her sweetness, while genuine, has also been a coping strategy developed in response to the narcissistic individuals in her life. Like mine and many others I work with, her journey shows that healing isn't just about survival.

I now understand that the trauma I endured is not my fault. But despite the shitty hands dealt, I fully believe it's my responsibility to heal—for myself, for my relationships, for the clients I have the privilege of serving, and for the future.

As I look back on my own long and painful healing journey, I have come to realize how little support there is for coping with the crippling confusion, pain, and trauma we endure. In hindsight, I now thank God for all my experiences, even including that painful "night" in my mother's car. I've channeled some pain into serving others and healing myself, striving to become the person I wish I'd had when I was younger. I approach this work from a place of peace rather than fear, insecurity, or resentment.

These experiences have imparted powerful and valuable life lessons. My experiences and healing journey have transformed me into a fully empowered, lovable, passionate, and resilient woman. Today, as a dedicated professional, wife, bonus mom, grandmother, published author, speaker, and therapist, I now embody the strength, authenticity, and vitality I once sought. What matters even more to me is using these experiences, along with extensive education and training, to help others heal from narcissistic abuse and sexual trauma.

I often tell clients that the key to breaking this cycle is moving beyond mere survival to a place of healing and growth. However, we must be safe first to do so. We can transform our lives and uncover our true selves by embracing our pain and seeking joy. Sarah's story is a powerful testament to this transformative journey, showing that healing and self-discovery are possible.

Seeking help is never easy, especially when we're accustomed to being the ones who 'help' others. That's why I offer virtual services—making it easier and more accessible for you to seek support wherever you feel most comfortable. While I may not have the chance to speak with everyone who reads this chapter, I want to share a few insights that have helped Sarah and countless other clients worldwide. These insights have contributed to their improved mental wellness, clarity, confidence, and healthier relationships on their healing journeys.

Trauma often comes from living under a cloud of confusion, self-doubt, and a relentless search for approval. It comes from seeking to fill a void left by distorted 'love' forms and not realizing that life can be different.

With that in mind, we might mistake pain for pleasure and not know any difference because someone led us to believe that our confusion, emptiness, longing, and pain are typical, often as a way to maintain control over us. But we must recognize that 'breadcrumbs' are no longer enough to sustain us. We deserve true pleasure!

At first glance, understanding psychological pleasure might seem trivial, but it's an essential part of recognizing what truly fulfills us. For those of us who have endured narcissistic abuse or sexual trauma, this understanding takes on profound significance. Once entangled in the demands and deceptions of others, pleasure can now be reclaimed and rediscovered on its own terms.

What constitutes pleasure for one person may differ vastly from another, and that's perfectly fine (as long as it doesn't harm you or others). The journey to understanding pleasure can indeed be overwhelming and confusing, but I promise you, it's worth it.

Once perceived in stark black and white, our world is a spectrum of colors—including 'shades of grey' in defining pleasure. For me, pleasure manifests in many forms now. I've learned to create my own joy, even in the most unexpected places. Despite facing multiple disabilities and pain conditions, I find satisfaction in proving past diagnoses and doubters wrong. I've achieved success, earning degrees with honors from top universities, even when others said I couldn't.

Today, I'm in a loving relationship with a wonderful, handsome, strong man who adores me (and I adore him). I'm far from being a 'drain on the system.' I've taken control of my life, but I continue to struggle with allowing myself to be fully seen by others— a challenge many survivors of narcissistic abuse know all too well.

So, how am I working to combat the urge to hide and make myself small? By writing this chapter, speaking locally and globally, and surprisingly, competing in international beauty pageants and competitions.

Finding empowerment through beauty pageants was something I never anticipated. I vividly recall preparing for the evening gown segment, wearing a dress my best friend and I designed. Right before stepping onto the stage, I joked to the backstage manager, 'I work with gangs, and this scares me more.' The fear was no joke—it was real and overwhelming. I had always found facing danger in my work easier than allowing others to see me entirely, but I pushed through, knowing it was a crucial part of my healing, even though it still scares the shit out of me (literally).

Hearing my husband's loud cheers from the audience reminded me exactly why I kept stepping into the spotlight despite the fear. The pride on his face during that moment still burns positively in my mind and warms my heart. It was a reminder that being seen and loved simultaneously was possible. Thank you, baby.

When I step into the spotlight, it's on my terms. I've chosen to be seen—not just for my beauty but for the strength and resilience shaped by my journey. Pageants have become a platform for me to raise awareness about influential women's and social issues, using my experiences with trauma and healing to inspire others. In every moment of fear, I remind myself that this visibility is a powerful part of my recovery—crown and all.

I also embrace my emotional and spiritual nature, knowing it brings pain and joy. I am grateful for the transformative events in my life. These experiences altered my path and empowered me to help thousands over nearly two decades. I channel my pain into advocacy, fuelled by the belief that life can improve, as I am a living testament to this truth.

Amid this journey, I've discovered that simple pleasures often provide the most profound satisfaction. Whether savoring a frothy chai latte with coconut milk, watching my playful dog chase birds in our backyard, or enjoying heartfelt conversations with loved ones over a home-cooked meal, these moments bring me genuine joy. The harmonious sounds of choirs, the vibrant energy of a marching band, and the delightful laughter of a baby all fill my heart with happiness.

Even small everyday joys can bring me some of the most profound pleasure. One of my favorites is seeing my beloved dog stick its head out of the car window to take in the sights and smells, which contribute to my well-being. This sight symbolizes freedom —something I never knew existed or thought possible. It brings a profound pleasure that resonates deep within the pit of my soul.

On a much deeper level, my journey to reclaim my sexuality has been transformative. Surviving narcissistic abuse and rape left me grappling with complex feelings about intimacy and trust. What once felt intimidating and vulnerable has gradually evolved into a source of profound comfort and fulfillment. Connecting with my spouse—emotionally, spiritually, and sexually—now represents a healing space where I experience genuine pleasure and safety. He has shown me that love does not hurt. This connection not only helps me reclaim a sense of control and empowerment but also reinforces my ability to enjoy intimacy in a way that once was overshadowed by past pain.

Do I still experience pain? Yes, I am human, just like you. However, pain and pleasure are not mutually exclusive. Finding pleasure amid pain is not about denying the hurt but about discovering joy, fulfillment, and purpose despite the challenges. For those of us who have faced deep trauma, embracing pleasure in all its forms is essential to the healing process.

In light of this, my commitment is to empower survivors on their healing journeys. If I can do it, so can you. While I often guide clients through these processes in sessions or coaching groups, here are a few suggestions to help you embark on your path toward healing, growth, and love:

1. **Accept and Acknowledge:** Accept what happened without agreeing with it or blaming yourself. Release the futile effort of fixing others and recognize that healing begins with acknowledging your pain.
2. **Seek the Right Help:** Therapy and a robust support system are essential. Both help you process your experiences and prepare you to support others without risking re-traumatization or burnout.
3. **Embrace Your Healing Journey:** As Dr. Ramani Durvasula wisely advises, "To go slow is to go fast." As survivors, we often rush through things, ignoring our needs (and pleasure) to serve others, which diminishes us. Take your time in seeking help and starting your recovery. Remember, there is no rush—your healing deserves the space to unfold at its own pace.

4. **Find Joy in Service:** Engaging in acts of service, like volunteering or mentoring, can be profoundly fulfilling. However, prioritize your healing first to make a meaningful impact on others' lives.
5. **Reconnect with Joy:** Rediscover activities that once brought you happiness, whether singing, spending time with loved ones, or engaging in hobbies that uplift you. Celebrate your victories, no matter how small, and permit yourself to experience a full range of emotions without judgment. Embracing joy is an essential part of your healing journey.
6. **Rediscover Healthy Sexuality:** Re-frame sex as something positive and empowering. Re-establish a healthy relationship with your sexuality, respecting your boundaries and desires. Healthy, consensual sexual relationships can be a powerful part of healing and rebuilding trust. Nothing is hotter than this!
7. **Balance Pain and Pleasure:** Recognize that pain and pleasure coexist. Embrace the full spectrum of the human experience and build a life that acknowledges struggles and triumphs.

While grief and pain may never entirely disappear, positive experiences can begin to outweigh the hurt over time. Healing takes effort, but it is possible. Relationships can be a powerful source of healing—if they're the right ones. You deserve to heal, grow, and experience genuine love.

After years of beauty pageants, earning certifications, facing health challenges, and navigating episodes of CPTSD, I've finally found myself in a healthy and fulfilling relationship. I now see myself and others with greater clarity. I hold no hatred; most importantly, I have learned to love myself. I aim to help others reach this same self-love and clarity.

My message is simple: You are imperfectly perfect, just as you are. You are worthy of healing and true love. The rainbows and butterflies may not come where you once expected, but you can create a new and fulfilling reality. It takes time, dedication, and the understanding that you can shape your life.

After over a decade of work and healing, I and my clients now find ourselves in healthy, loving relationships. My spouse and I, brought together by our traumas, support each other's healing. The tattoo on my back, a quote from Carl Jung —"I am not what happened to me; I am what I choose to become"—is a constant reminder of my journey and the power of resilience. Whenever I feel my partner's loving touch, it reminds me of warmth, protection, and joy beyond pain.

Wishing you peace and happy healing.

About the Author
Malissa Veroni-Prince

Malissa Veroni-Prince is a Canadian renowned specialist in therapeutic interventions for narcissistic abuse and sexual trauma. With over 15 years of experience as a respected therapist, mentor, published author, podcast guest, keynote speaker, and former university instructor, she dedicates her time to helping adults break free from the constraints of trauma. Through her transformative approach—combining advanced therapeutic techniques, personalized coaching, and educational resources—Malissa empowers survivors to reclaim their power, achieve profound healing, and thrive in all aspects of life. She also creates and nurtures supportive online communities to encourage ongoing growth and meaningful connections.

Outside of her professional work, Malissa finds joy in life's simple pleasures: spending time with her family and cherished dog, enjoying great food, exploring new destinations, immersing herself in music, and pursuing personal growth. Her mission is to inspire global healing, resilience, and lasting joy.

https://linktr.ee/malissaveroniprince

Chapter Eight
The Taboo Female Body: The Power of Our Cycles

By Sierra Melcher

Reclaiming Our Bodies

This book wouldn't have existed without my daughter asking me a powerful question. She was eight, and one day in the kitchen, she asked, "How old will I be when I get my period?"

I asked if any of her friends talked about it. She said no. We discussed why women have a period and how and when we can have babies.

She asked, *"Why are there so many basic things that we don't talk about?"*

"Great question," I said. *"Some topics are considered taboo, and society teaches us not to discuss them, regardless of how universal or fundamentally human they are."*

"Well, that's dumb," she wisely stated.

I have always been open with her about my bleeding cycle to demystify this natural human process intentionally. I told her that there wasn't an exact age. But I had to grow into that understanding and comfort with my body and cycle; I discovered a lot later in life. **The female body, and particularly the menstrual cycle, has been misunderstood, underappreciated, and often vilified.** It was indeed a journey.

I grew up with the societal story that my menstruation was an inconvenience and a female burden that should be masked in any way possible. So I internalized knowing as little about how my body worked as possible and vehemently disconnecting my sense of self from my body... I was my mind. I was things I could control and intellectualize. For most days of the month, I could almost pretend I was male. I bled for a few days, challenging my attempt to reject my femaleness. I had nearly perfected it.

My daughter likely would not exist without my previous ignorance of the power of my bodily cycles. Seventh-grade sex ed. never taught me about my cycle; it only preached abstinence... and once I had abandoned that, I was left to my own defenses.

My pregnancy forced me to learn how that happened... I went back and watched all the movies they showed in middle school and marveled at the impossibility of it—the unlikelihood of a single sperm finding a viable egg and creating a new life. It unraveled all my curiosity about how I had been riding this wild ride all these years without even knowing, putting so much energy into negating my natural flux.

The birth of my daughter further convinced me of the undeniable power and creative force of the female body. In the following years, I learned and discovered an ancient and recently reclaimed understanding that accepting and **embracing the menstrual cycle is essential to personal empowerment and collective female strength.**

It has claimed a fundamental role in how I support authors in writing their books. It informs how I run my business and life, and I teach it widely, primarily to women who have a front-row seat to this powerful cycle but also to men who have their unique cyclical nature.

I now regularly state without shame or embarrassment to my male friends, " I got my period yesterday ..." to just bring this regular occurrence to the conversation the same way they might mention having a cough or going for a run. I have found the response extraordinary (a non-thing sometimes, and others met with support or even curiosity).

The Historical Suppression of the Female Body

Menstruation historically has been taboo across many cultures.

Intentional disempowerment of women meant separating them from their powerful cyclical nature. Patriarchy **has diminished the value of female bodies and their cycles.**

Let's review some myths and misbeliefs around menstruation to understand the adverse effects on self-image and body perception. (Here are just a few.)

1. Menstruation as "Dirty" or "Impure"
• **Myth**: *Menstruating women are considered "unclean" or "impure," and in some cultures, they are even isolated or restricted from certain activities during their periods.*
• **Effect**: This perpetuates feelings of shame and embarrassment around menstruation, leading women to hide this natural process and feel disconnected from their bodies. It reinforces the idea that something inherently normal is "wrong" or "disgusting," contributing to poor self-esteem.

2. Periods Are a Curse or Punishment
• **Myth**: *Menstruation is often seen as a curse or punishment (historically linked to religious narratives such as Eve's "sin" in the Garden of Eden.)*
• **Effect**: This narrative positions the menstrual cycle as something to be endured rather than embraced, fostering a negative relationship with one's body. It can lead women to view their biology as burdensome and undesirable, perpetuating the belief that their bodies are inherently flawed.

3. Emotional Instability as a Sign of Weakness
• **Myth**: *The belief that women are "overly emotional" or irrational*

during their menstrual cycles, particularly during PMS, is often used to discredit women's feelings and actions.
• **Effect**: This myth dismisses the complexity of emotions women experience and pathologizes natural emotional fluctuations. Women may internalize this belief, doubting their feelings and viewing themselves as unstable or less capable, which can harm self-worth and confidence.

4. Menstrual Pain Is Normal and Should Be Silently Endured
• **Myth**: *The assumption that period pain is normal and should be accepted without complaint leads many women to suffer through conditions like endometriosis or fibroids without seeking medical attention.*
• **Effect**: This myth minimizes women's health concerns, making them feel as if their pain is not valid or important. The result can be feelings of powerlessness and frustration with their bodies, leading to further disconnection and mistrust of their physical experiences.

5. Menstruation Equals Weakness
• **Myth**: *The idea that menstruation makes women physically weaker or less capable (both mentally and physically) contributes to the notion that women are not suited for specific roles or responsibilities, especially in male-dominated fields.*
• **Effect**: This belief undermines women's sense of capability and strength, fostering the idea that, to be taken seriously, they need to "push through" or hide their menstrual experiences. It creates an environment where women must suppress their natural cycles, affecting their self-perception and professional confidence.

Understanding the Menstrual Cycle: A Source of Power

I am teaching my daughter to be cyclically literate about her body and each phase's energetic needs and power. I periodically break down the four phases of the menstrual cycle (menstrual, follicular, ovulation, luteal) and explain what happens in each phase, both physically and emotionally, using my own experience as the template and context until she has her own experience to build from.

I emphasize how each phase offers unique strengths and insights:

- **Menstrual phase:** Reflection, rest, and renewal.
- **Follicular phase:** Creativity, energy, and new beginnings.
- **Ovulation phase:** Connection, communication, and magnetic energy.
- **Luteal phase:** Inner strength, productivity, and intuition.

I particularly love how this natural rhythm aligns with seasons, lunar phases, or even project cycles, fostering harmony when understood and embraced. (In fact my next book is all about this.) So much of this process is subtle and internal; without a framework for observing and embodying, it can be overlooked. The external world we have been taught to witness is an easier reference to begin integrating the cyclical nature of all things. Whether you live in the tropics or the more temperate zones, the concept of the seasons is well understood. The moon is a constant reminder that you can look to the sky on any given night and get a snapshot of this constant cyclical nature... that's no accident synchs perfectly with the average 28-day menstruation cycle. Is that pure coincidence? I think not.

Embracing the Cycle: Shifting Perspectives

Thanks to the work of incredible women, I could learn and integrate a new relationship with my body and my cyclical nature. I read books by Dr. Clarissa Pinkola Estes, Raine Eilser, Pucy H Pearce, Sharon Blackie, Chimamanda Ngozi Adichie, and Regina Thomashouer, to name just a few. They awakened my curiosity and burgeoning awareness and led me deeper. I studied with Lisa Lister, who made the connection for me between my cycle and my productivity and creativity. That was a revolutionary breakthrough.

Growing up, I had an intermittent and sporadic cycle. I never tracked it because sometimes six months would pass between cycles. I was diagnosed with polycystic ovaries and told I would never be able to have children. I disconnected and just endured my period when it came randomly.

I didn't have an intimate relationship with my body in any regard. I had poor eating habits and struggled with an eating disorder, bulimia, through middle school and high school. I didn't exercise and thought I could ignore my body.

I became fitter by moving more and eating better. Surprisingly, my cycle regulated itself, becoming reliable between 29 and 31 days. I started to track and anticipate the unavoidable element: the blood.

Once aware of the rhythmic element... I could also start to see the shifts during the cycle.

Stunned by the benefits of paying attention to the cycle—increased productivity, better mental health, improved relationships, and deeper self-awareness—I fully committed and talked to anyone and everyone who would listen despite this remaining a taboo topic in most contexts.

Whether you are tracking or "cycle syncing" (eating, exercising, and scheduling life in accordance with your cycle), there are many insights to discover.

Body Literacy: The Language of Our Bodies

In my first book, **How Change Really Happens**, I shared what I had put together: the brilliant connection between the natural world and how we grow and evolve. For years, I was disconnected from my most essential nature, my own body. I tried to live outside of nature's laws, which was exhausting. Realizing I am just as much part of the systems that govern the universe, the seasons, and the moon's rotation allows me to soften and trust; this alone replenishes and diverts much wasted energy.

The most significant part of this has been body literacy: the ability to understand and interpret signals from your body. Our female bodies have a massive database of information that, once plugged into, can inform and guide all decisions. Not only up-leveling our productivity and creativity but more so in a way that downgrades our anxiety and stress. The modern pervasive disconnection from the body leads to issues like stress, burnout, and hormonal imbalance for many women. We are running full-steam ahead and operating well beyond our capacity, not because we are incapable but because we have lost the knowledge that rest and reflection are powerful fundamental keys to our creative productivity. Developing body literacy allows women to take control of their health and promote balance and empowerment. From there, it is an easy and logical step to calm, peaceful creation.

I want to live in this reality and raise my daughter to claim it for herself boldly. Of course, I am sharing my experience and awareness with her to make that happen. Still, moreover, there needs to be a more significant cultural shift so the pervasive dominant story doesn't skew her to unconsciousness regarding her body and cyclical nature.

Healing the Relationship with the Female Body

Many related topics could be their own chapters in the next Taboo book: struggles many women face with body image, menstruation, and reproductive health. Reclamation tools and practices for embracing the female body are also still taboo in some regards: meditation, journaling, yoga, herbal support, yoni massage, and education about menstrual health.

If I had been connected with my body and my cycle, I would have known that unprotected sex 14 days after my previous period would likely lead to pregnancy, yet it came as a bit of a surprise. My pregnancy taught me more about my body and the power of my creative cycles than anything else. Since then, I have been highly tuned-in and have continuously learned from and alongside my body.

I am grateful for my previous ignorance because it gifted me with my daughter. At the same time, I wonder how my 20s and 30s could have been different if I had been raised to embrace and harness the power of my cyclical nature rather than trying to force myself into a linear and constant showing up like a man...

I am grateful for the last ten years that have taught me how much more productive I can be by harnessing the flux of my energy and creative capacity:

- Creating a human
- Writing and publishing many books
- Starting and running several businesses
- Thriving in a female body
- Looking forward to the cyclical flux and making the most of it

A Tool for Feminine Leadership

It feels like cognitive dissonance to think that female leadership is dependent on our cyclical nature because, for so long, we were taught that was a weakness we had to hide, negate, and overcome. Leveraging your menstrual cycle can enhance leadership and success, particularly for women in business, education, or any field.

Women can harness their cyclical power to lead and create more intuitively, effectively, and compassionately. I often ask, "What if it were fun?" That is not our current perception. We still think it must be hard, but we can play when we harness the cycles.

To repeat and deepen the awareness of the phases and the capacity available to us in each phase of the cycle:

- **The menstrual phase** *invites reflection, rest, and renewal directed to find the inspiration for the next cycle in your writing or business.*
- **The follicular phase** *is characterized by creativity, energy, and new beginnings. It is the ideal time to plan your next project or adventure.*
- **The ovulation phase** *is characterized by connection, communication, and magnetic energy. During this phase, speaking on stage, presenting, teaching, and writing are most natural.*
- **The luteal phase** *aligns with Inner strength, productivity, and intuition and, as such, is a perfect time to review and revise to find room for iteration and improvement. PMS deems us cranky and irritable. When focused, this highly*

critical energy can also be productive for identifying injustice and ways to grow.

We use this awareness to fuel our creative writing, publishing & business leadership cycle. For example, people are often stunned at the growth of Red Thread Publishing in the past three and a half years; with the tiny team, we have published 56 of 57 bestselling books. I regularly hear comments like, "It takes most companies nearly ten years to do what you have done in three." It is reasonable to ask how, as a single mother*, I have been able to do that, write three books, and contribute to 14 others. The answer is simple, and I know you know it by now: by harnessing the power of my cyclical nature, I have become incredibly imaginative, creative, and productive. I have become much more impactful than ever by enforcing a mandatory rest cycle.

> **I am aware that single motherhood is a spectrum. My version of single motherhood is defined by zero participation or support, financial or otherwise, from my daughter's father. This is simply shared to highlight the responsibility I carry and, in part, despite and in part because I have become fiercely productive ... as much as I am fiercely committed to my rest and play - as the essential key to all of my success.*

In the TED Masterclass I recently participated in, I started my talk by asking, "What if a nap was the key to your next breakthrough?"

Burnout is the likely outcome of following the cultural drive we are all raised with to be in constant show-up mode. I have dabbled with burnout earlier in life. I let the dominant narrative direct my energy. That only got me so far, and entirely at my own expense.

Now, I help women understand how they change, seeing how each phase we live has a purpose and function. When aligned and aware of these phases, we can be potent creative leaders. The direct opposite of what we are taught becomes the key to the impact and well-being we crave.

Empowering Future Women (the Next Generation)

We can certainly change this story and make menstruation not a taboo topic for the next generation, but for that to work, we have to do the unraveling work within ourselves first and foremost.

- Let your cycle be observed. Don't hide it away.
- Teach young girls about their bodies and the power of their menstrual cycles early on.
- Reframe menstruation as a gift rather than a burden.
- Share actionable steps for promoting body literacy in schools, families, and communities.

If it is a stretch to do this with our daughters, start with your dearest friends, especially if it is uncomfortable. I let my daughter watch me drain and clean my Luna cup from an early age. It is a natural process, and I want her to learn to be comfortable with it rather than dread it.

The physical process is undoubtedly part of it; the emotional and energetic flux is another part. As she approaches her preteens, we strap in for the hormonal and emotional roller coaster ahead. I can't preach how to get through that, as it is still on the horizon.

However, I assure you that I will share more of my emotional and creative process with her as I do with my author community. I will give language to the phases and share my experiences.

"Sometimes a nap is how I show up for my next book or business." My days off are required for the next push or creative insight. Likewise, there are weeks when I am on fire with energy and ideas, overwhelmed with enthusiasm, and overcommitted. I have to be careful not to be lulled into high delivery all the time, remembering that downtime is as powerful as uptime.

Coming Home to Ourselves

Whether you are motivated by your physical or mental well-being, whether you are driven to be a leader in your work or family, whether you are looking to heal your body from feminine wounds or support the future women in your life, it is time to remove the taboo of menstruation. Not only is it an unnecessary burden, it is an unimaginable ease and acceptance, a wealth of creativity, and potent productivity.

Embracing the menstrual cycle and your female body as a source of power, wisdom, and connection is the fast track to unlocking your next level of impact.

I founded Red Thread Publishing with the deliberate intention of supporting more women in having a voice in the world. That is much more than writing and publishing, although that is a fundamental part. Without tapping into our capacity and aligning with our natural energy, we cannot likely do this... If we do it from the traditional place of self-depletion, we arrive at the goal drained and empty. This is not the way.

It is part of our ethos and a fundamental part of how I run my business and my life. I make space for my cyclical nature and encourage the women on my team and the authors we support to do the same as a way of growing. Even while I practice what I preach, I still stumble and fall into old ways but quickly feel the consequences of being misaligned. It is a brilliant reminder to embrace and honor each phase of the cycle.

Reclaim your relationship with your body, celebrate every aspect of the menstrual cycle, and support other women in doing the same. Understanding our cycles can help us lead more fulfilling, fun, and empowered lives.

About the Author
Sierra Melcher

Award-winning and Best-selling author, international speaker & educator Sierra Melcher is the founder of **Red Thread Publishing LLC.** *(home of Red Thread Books & Red Falcon Press).* She leads an all-female publishing company with a mission to support 10,000 women to become successful published authors & thought leaders. Offering world-class coaching & courses that focus on community, collaboration, and a uniquely feminine approach at every stage of the authoring process.

Sierra has a Master's degree in education and has spoken & taught around the world. Originally from the United States, Sierra lives in Medellin, Colombia, with her young daughter.

instagram.com/redthreadbooks
linkedin.com/in/sierra-melcher
amazon.com/author/sierramelcher
goodreads.com/sierra-melcher

Chapter Nine
Carving Trails in Your Heart

By Kelly Upton Jameson

In Loving Memory

I died last week. I took my own life; it was time. So much of my life became taboo. Even my death is taboo.

What's needed... truth, messiness, weirdness, creative work, and resistance...

Like so many people, at one time, I defined myself by my job, my partner, and my abilities. But then I got sick and was diagnosed with multiple sclerosis (MS). I couldn't do my job anymore. My marriage fell apart. My illness took so much from me—so many things I loved I could no longer do. It was hard to know who I was anymore. But I lived more fully than any doctor or professional told me I could. In unexpected ways, my illness gifted me a version of life, a version of myself I would have never otherwise known.

My illness forced me to make some unconventional decisions. Joyfully, yet weepingly, I got divorced. I no longer belonged to my father, husband, or any man. To die as *his* wife was not living. It was defining me inaccurately. I needed to feel life without being under the control of a man before I died. Even if for a brief time, I needed to do what *I wanted* every second of every breathing moment left inside my decaying body.

As I grew up, I continuously did as I was told. I wore the *correct* outfit. I was friends with the *right* people. I said all the *accepted* words formed into *appropriate* sentences.

But at this critical point in my life, I decided that I was going to see the world, converse *with anyone about anything,* hear stories of people's lives, *feel* their lives, their love, and their pain, and wrap it all around me.

After 11 years of various hospitals and specialists, tests, and treatments, my remaining hopeless time was dedicated to international travel. Finally, I was going to live and die on my terms.

Retired /Disabled

I want to share a bit of the back story. The MS Society asked me to share my story with other MSers, but I'm choosing to share it with you. Here is what I have to say about it.

Diagnosis: When my test results came in, my primary care doctor said to leave work and get to the hospital to meet with a neurologist. He told me my Multiple Sclerosis diagnosis, gave me three meds to research, and out the door I went.

I called my parents on the way back to work. Their attorney said to tell no one at work. "They wouldn't want to keep you," they said. We are often told to keep our weaknesses a secret. I couldn't do that.

Instead, I went to work and told my boss. He suggested I go home, but I wanted to work. My hand pain was intense. I couldn't make it through the day without colleagues massaging my hands. They took turns each day, which got me through!

When I moved to Macomb, I needed a new job. I interviewed with the boss. I told him I had MS. He found out insurance would cover my expenses. He hired me despite my disease. I didn't want to work with a company or people who didn't accept me. So many people helped me. They filed paperwork to take care of me when I got sick from the feeling of fireworks going off all through my body.

New symptoms came and went but mostly stayed.

- Stabbing pain in my hands. *I asked the Mayo Clinic to try amputation. They refused.*
- Blurred vision
- Cognitive impairments- thinking, learning, memory loss, judgments and making decisions trouble, trouble concentrating and understanding, solving problems, simple math, and word loss
- Feeling pain *where I thought my insides were going to fall out of my vagina*
- Loss of bowel control
- Constipation resulting in numerous tests and hospital visits
- Spasticity- muscle weakness
- Fatigue: causing me to sleep 20 hours a day
- Fainting, dizziness
- Heat and cold intolerances
- Poor balance
- Vertigo
- Lack of coordination- walking into walls and doors
- Falling everywhere. In the middle of the streets.
- Anxiety, mood swings, depression
- Bee sting feelings on my legs, arms, and face. Burning skin
- Reduced sensation in my fingers and feet
- Hearing loss

A doctor told me I shouldn't have children – I got a hysterectomy.

I was told I couldn't travel – I traveled through Europe, Africa, and South America.

I was told I couldn't live in a Spanish-speaking country, so I lived in Colombia for years.

I was told I needed a nursing home – I would leave my apartment in Medellin and forget where I was, where I was going, and how to get home. Strangers would take my sheet of paper with my address and walk me home.

Tell me I can't do something. *I'll do it.*

Because of the changing symptoms, I felt I had to start over again repeatedly. But I won't give up. MS tipped my life upside down. I struggle with people seeing only a snippet of my day, thinking I'm fine. But I hold my head up and march forward. I have MS; MS doesn't have me.

―――

Travel

"Travel is the only way to be lost and found at the same time...."

— Brenna Smith.

I gave myself two years to feel repetitive culture shock, experience everything unfamiliar, and meet *new-not-allowed-before* people while writing a book to leave behind when I'm gone. I wanted the world to understand physical yet invisible pain, depression, multiple sclerosis, and suicide.

My illness didn't take away my ability to dream of untraditional and unlikely paths for a disabled woman, but it did create numerous obstacles for travel. *There are always solutions.* As I found inspirational humans fighting their pain, I learned our diagnoses are irrelevant, even if they're permanent. Accepting pain by taking the time to know what could make you move past it can change your path.

How could I manage to realize these dreams? The answer is often in a place we would least expect it. I hired a tour guide and purchased a one-way ticket to Barcelona, Spain. We traveled through Europe and ended up in South America. Colombia was the best place for suicide, I had decided.

My Illness taught me to take fierce ownership of my life and my choices.

Try to travel; otherwise

you may become racist,
and you may end up believing
that your skin is the only one
to be right,
that your language
is the most romantic
and that you were the first
to be the first.
...
Travel,
because traveling teaches to resist,
not to depend,
to accept others, not just for who they are
but also for what they can never be.
To know what we are capable of,
to feel part of a family
beyond borders,
beyond traditions and culture.
Traveling teaches us to be beyond.
...

— GIO EVAN, POET AND SONGWRITER.
TRANSLATED FROM ITALIAN.

"Do not follow where the path may lead. Go instead where there is no path and leave a trail."

— RALPH WALDO EMERSON.

While traveling, the greatest joys are the people you meet. Open yourself to meet new people and breathe their stories as your own. Listen to their words and absorb their motivation.

> Once in a while, if you are lucky, a person can leave a trail in your heart that inspires you to leap from your current path and go toward the unknown.
> I met a woman today who inspired me to challenge myself through her progress in life. She reminded me of a dear friend I lost a year ago.
> Thank you for leaving a trail through my heart.
> I listened, I heard, and I'm ready.
> Women travelers. Wanderers who are far from lost.
>
> — *Girls Love Travel*

It was a life unimaginable to me. So I took my passport and set off to explore. It wasn't what I saw along the way. It was who I met. Their life experiences, mixed with mine, brought a new understanding.

I would have been nothing without them. My understanding of life came alive by sharing our painful memories and memories that kept us alive to pursue a life we dreamed of, a life we deserved. Understanding where someone comes from, what they survived, and how similar we all are. Those are the most essential pages found between the pages of our passports. Never forget those who help you see light in a world of darkness.

The world is much smaller than we think. From travel and connecting with people, I learned how amazingly synchronized the world can be–

Writing My Book

I always wanted to write my story but never did. Now is my chance.

I had sketched out an entire book that would never come to be. This chapter is all I leave.

I wrote to my editor:

> I definitely want a memoir. I want this to be my life story. It's important to have happened and be true to connect with MS survivors.

We drafted the scope of my book; this is what we came up with.
My book Synopsis:

Right to Die: An Adventure to End a Lifetime
She set out on a trip she knew would be her last, determined to end it all, but it is the journey, not the destination.
A real and potent exploration of disease, dying, and the choices we make about how to live life fully. One young woman traveled as her dying wish.
1) the problem in the market for the target reader,
2) the solution your book has for them,
3) why you're the one to write it.
plot twist
A true story written as fiction.

More messages with my editor:

> The story is very much alive!

> Great! I can't wait to work on this with you.

> Hi. I thought it was time to talk. I'm devastated. I spoke with my insurance agent—if I write a book or make an income, they will take away my health insurance and income.

LOST

But what do you do when you don't know who you are, what value you bring, and when the future seems to hold more pain than promise? I know this sounds depressing, but it's not. I struggled with mental health—there were many times I felt like I couldn't go on living because of the physical and emotional pain. Ironically, it was some of the world's most horrific injustices that kept me alive and fighting for so long. And yet, despite everything, I lived a wonderful and incredibly blessed life. I traveled more than most people ever will. I got to see the world in spectacular ways. I struggled, yes, but I also tasted so much of life—dancing, eating, befriending people, and learning valuable lessons.

People may not understand my choices. They might even be angry with me and have every right to be. My choices to travel were my own. My choice to end my life was equally my choice.

One of the things I've learned through all this is that the concern about what people think doesn't just go away. I still worry about how others perceive my life, especially my death. I'm judging and weighing every word in this chapter because I don't want to upset anyone or cause problems. But I've also learned that it's impossible to live a whole life inside that safe space without upsetting someone or going against someone else's beliefs and values. We can let our parents, friends, culture, children, environment, and expectations stifle us, make us small, hold us back, and keep us pretending. Letting these taboos cage us in until there's no space left—not for me, not for you, not for anything real. Because what one person finds taboo, another may see as freedom from restriction.

> The way people view you.
> Sometimes, I think about the different characters I play
>   in everybody's story.
> I'm a terrible person in some people's narratives and a
>   Godsend in others.
> And none of it has anything to do with the person I
>   truly am.
> The lens that others view you through is colored by
>   their upbringing, beliefs, and individual experiences.
> Some people see your bright personality as endearing,
>   and others see it as annoying.

> Some people think you're weak and emotional, and others feel safe to be themselves around you.
> ...
> And none of it has to do with who you truly are as a person.
> What you have to understand is that you have no authority over how people view you, so never try to control the way others see you because the only thing that truly matters when the dust settles down at the end of the day is what you genuinely see in yourself.
>
> — CODY BRET

Hope

You will find the energy to change. You will feel the exhaustion fade. You will leave the concrete block that held you in a dark place. And you will find people willing to give you the chance to be the person your mental illness prevented you from being.

I tried to be this person for others and myself. *It is easier with others.*

I was stumbling. You knew it. I listened to you. But, I wish I had stayed with you to continue rising. From the streets of Barcelona, Spain, to Cape Verde. A crying girl, you turned into a solid woman. I am better for having known you. Thank you. You did leave me with one of the best parts of you... I will shine, fly, laugh, and cry because I have your love. I will hurt. I will heal. I will continue to fall. But I can get up now. Your love shines on in everyone who knew you. We are enough. We are plenty.

I have lost so many dear friends. Some to MS and some to domestic violence. May all of the people who have endured the pain of domestic abuse find peace before it's too late. Missing you.

Advice from a friend:

1. Stay silly.
2. Adventure seriously.
3. Live curiously.

> *These friends of mine are brave, faithful, beautiful, strong, and encouraging. You are my light. What a beautiful life I've lived because of you.*
> **To my brave friend,**
> *What a beautiful thing to watch you put one foot in front of the other and keep going when quitting would've been easier. Your courage is contagious, and your commitment—inspires me daily to step into the light and shine. Thank you for being you.*
> **To my faithful friend,**
> *You've been there for every season. You've danced with me in the sun and held my hand in the rain. You've never left me or quit me. You don't have to reply to every text or answer every call for me to know you'll show up when I need you most. We've been through so much together, and I can't imagine my life without you standing next to me.*
> **To my beautiful friend,**
> *I wish you could see yourself through my eyes. I wish you weren't so hateful towards yourself and those voices didn't lie to you. You're not perfect, but you're pretty great to those of us who know you best. You're worthy as you are. You're enough today. You don't need to lose*

weight, have the right clothes, or fix yourself up to shine. Believe me, the world is better when you show up just as you are.

To my strong friend,
You could've given up, but you didn't. You could've buckled under the pressure or grown silent under the criticism. You could've stopped, but you keep showing up. You know what you have to offer, and you know exactly who you are. If you need to rest, I'm here. And if you need a space to vent and relax, I'm here too. You carry it so well, and it is admirable to watch you climb those mountains, but please know that I'll lift your burdens and lighten the load. I know it's heavy, but I love you. You don't have to be strong alone.

To my encouraging friend,
Your words. They've lifted me more times than I can count. They've made me fly. They've made me believe. They helped me breathe when I wasn't sure my lungs had enough air. Your actions. They've carried me through. They've made me stand taller. They've held my hand and made me go out and feel the sunshine again—and how sweet it felt. Thank you for spurring me on. For pushing, pulling, and opening my eyes to all the hope and beauty there is to see.

Love,
Me

Many of you know the complications that come with multiple sclerosis. I am lucky. Multiple sclerosis has shown me what's important and who I want to be. But MS progresses, and no one knows what's to come tomorrow.

More beautiful than before. How suffering transforms us:

Messages to a friend:

> filling out forms for insurance, my lawyer and neurologist. Fun times

> Sending you the best. Anything I can do?

> I'm 'sick' again. The gastroenterologist told me to go to the ER, but I'm trying to wait to see if this might pass. I haven't slept in days because my back pain radiates down my legs, and my stomach is almost unbearable.

> I have something difficult to tell you. I tried to jump off a bridge last week, and I've been in the hospital for a week now. They took away my phone, but I'm out as of last night. We will spend all of Friday in Iowa to give me a break from Illinois. So I'm sorry to say I need to reschedule again. It's been a rough couple of weeks, but I'm back.

> I'm suicidal again and have tried medication, psychiatrist, psychologist, inpatient programs, and Ketamine therapy. I heard Ayahuasca helps with depression.

We spend so much time concerned with what others think or need from us that the better we are at that, the less space we have to figure out who we are and what we want to do with this one precious life. But I'm going to say it, and maybe you won't agree—and that's fine—but what we each do with our lives is uniquely and entirely our own. My choices were mine alone. That's not to say I wish my choices didn't hurt anyone —I do; I hate that my choices caused pain. But in the end, they were my choices because it was my life.

Did I want my life to be different? Absolutely —sometimes a thousand times a day. But we each work with what we've got, whether it's a chronic illness, divorce, career change, neurodiversity, depression, inequality, injustice, or financial struggles—we all just do what we can. I'm so grateful and so lucky because even though my life did end in suicide, **it's not the defining factor of who I am.** It's not the defining factor of the life I lived. The fact that some of you think I died too soon says more about you than it does about me. I want to remind you that we each have this precious life. We're all going to die—it's terrifying and uncomfortable to think about, but it's the truth. We don't all have control over when or how we die, but we do have control over how we live.

Do you know how I lived? I lived fully. I laughed a lot. I made friends worldwide, learning and connecting and leaving my mark, bringing a piece of each of those people with me. I have some regrets in life—who doesn't?—***but I never regretted an adventure.*** I never regretted taking a risk, making a new friend, or saying hi to a stranger on the street. My story isn't meant to persuade or convince you of anything—I know no one can lead your life but you. My story is to share, and if I can encourage you just a little bit to live fuller, to live braver, in total awareness that your life will end but that today is probably not that day, then go live it boldly.

One of the things I love is that every person I've ever met, every person I've befriended in every place I've traveled, I've left a little bit of myself with them—a bit of a treasure, a reminder. And you know, that's all we can ever hope for—that our lives can touch and impact another life, that we connect and support one another. I know I've done my part and can rest easy on that knowledge. When I was with people, I was really *with* them—present and loving. And for that, I'm proud.

All the women I have been are proud of the woman I have become, even now.

I had always dreamed of dying amongst the birds and lush nature of Colombia. Eventually, due to medical necessities, I had to leave Colombia and return to the US for a brain scan. Then, the pandemic hit and prevented me from ever returning. Then, I received a final unexpected miracle. I fell in love. With this man, I became a stepmom to two wonderful children. It was all a gift. But my body and mind had progressed too far. The physical and emotional pain became too much, and I had to make my exit. Grateful for it all.

Now, all that remains of me is in the hearts of the people I knew and loved, and in these pages. And that is enough.

About the Author
Kelly Upton Jameson

OBITUARY

Kelly A. Upton Jameson, 46, of Vermont, IL, formerly of Clarendon Hills, IL, passed away on Thursday, July 4, 2024, at her residence. She was born May 4, 1978, in Hinsdale, IL, to Wesley P. Upton of Downers Grove, IL and Polly Upton of Macomb, IL.

Kelly is survived by her parents; brother Charles W. "Chuck" Upton of Willowbrook, IL; Big Brothers Big Sisters™ Niyesha T. Booker of Macomb, IL; partner and love Joshua Whitney Mercer of Vermont, IL; his children Sydney, Noah, Jonas, and Ben Mercer of Vermont, IL; and special friends Kelly met on her travels throughout the United States, Europe, Africa, Mexico, and Colombia.

Kelly graduated from Hinsdale Central High School in 1996, attended Western Illinois University, and graduated in 2000 with a BA in Psychology. She lived a very active life and enjoyed helping others.

By Kelly Upton Jameson

Before moving to Vermont, IL, Kelly lived in Medellin, Colombia, where she volunteered to teach English, helped feed displaced families from Venezuela, and fought for justice for her dear friend Kelly Knight.

Publisher's Note:

Kelly was a dear friend of mine. While she was alive, we planned to write her book. Bringing this story to life to honor and remember her while sharing her light and wisdom is the best way to fulfill her wish to write and publish. This chapter is an interweaving of conversations, emails, social media posts and more. It is in her own words as much as possible. I hope I have done her justice.

With love, Sierra Melcher

Chapter Ten
What Will People Think?

By Anonymous

We have a million excuses for why we are afraid to remove our masks of perfection and show the world our true selves. What's up with that?

I was feeling brave and ready to face my demons and tell my secrets finally. I committed to writing a chapter for *Taboo*. Finally, I thought I could relax and be at peace after letting it all out. I struggled, wrote, rewrote, edited, and finally finished the darn thing.

I consider myself a good person, a woman who is strong, confident, and psychologically healthy.

But after completing my chapter, a disturbing thing happened: I didn't feel the relief I expected. Instead, I started feeling very uncomfortable. Suddenly, I realized I was being **slammed with shame**. Oops, I'm not done with my psychological healing, I guess!

The voices started:

> *You are -*
> *A terrible person,*
> *such a disappointment,*

> *selfish,*
> *wild,*
> *a promiscuous slut,*
> *unfaithful,*
> *adulterer,*
> *bad child,*
> *bad wife,*
> *bad mother...*

...the voices of judgment were loud and harsh. I hurt a lot of people. I didn't honor my promises or fulfill my obligations. I didn't do *what I was supposed to do!*

What will people think of me?

You, dear reader, will no doubt have your own version of this voice. I suspect we may have more in common than we think.

I took a risk and asked my sister, who's a writer, to give the chapter a beta read. I agonized for days when I didn't hear back from her. Was she so horrified by what I wrote that she wouldn't love me anymore? Was what I shared unforgivable? It was a horrible day or two in my head. Then I realized I had not actually hit send, so she had never gotten my chapter at all. It's clear how my projections led to fear - for no reason. (And by the way, after she read it, she approvingly deemed it "very brave.")

This entire process has been very illuminating... yet it has rattled me. We should share trust and all the Brené Brown vulnerabilities stuff more openly. I do. I think so, but there are still some things that I am too uncomfortable to share here or anywhere.

I am unsure what is more brutal, navigating what other people will think or what I think of who I have been and what I have done.

I have heard all the excuses... in my head and from other women writers I have had the honor of knowing over the years:

- "I can share my story when my parents are dead."
- "I can only share my story when I am dead."

- "I can only share my story anonymously."
- "I will share my story when I leave the country so I don't have to deal with my dad's disappointment in person."
- "I can't write my real story because my kids will not respect me."
- "I can't share the truth because my partner will leave me."
- "If I tell the truth about my abortion, what will my kid/partner/parents think?"
- "I can't tell *all* my story; it is still too raw" (after 40 years).
- "If I tell that part of who I am, people won't look at me the same."

I know I am not the only one. This devastating fear to share, fed by shame, does not make me special or unique. Tragically, it is what unites me with so many others.

It is not just a cute fridge magnet that states, "For most of history, Anonymous was a woman." It is true and continues to this day. The historical culture that prevented women from writing and speaking publicly was undoubtedly part of it. Still, I see that more than a change of politics and culture is needed to turn the natural, cultural tide. I grew up in the height of the modern feminist revolution. It is not just about rights, education, and financial independence... all those are powerful and, thank goodness, more available than in the past. I have more rights and freedoms than any woman in history. Yet there is still more... It is about permission to be myself. I am working on it.

In this process, I have realized that it is one thing to do personal work; it is quite another to commit it to print and share it with the world.

In the end, here is what I decided.

First, I forgive myself and love myself completely. I feel for the lost girl I was when I made some of my missteps. I honor her journey to freedom and self-awareness. I even love the more mature me who has continued to make mistakes later in life when I should have known better.

Second, many genuinely love me and accept my darkness and

considerable light. I am blessed by their understanding and companionship on my journey.

And lastly, for those inclined to judge me and my choices, I say: you have no right to intimate knowledge of me. It's none of your damn business how I led my life, and so I choose not to share my struggles and triumphs with you. And that's OK.

For now, I will keep my secrets to myself.

It is up to me to determine how I feel about my life choices, both the bold and brave ones and the mistakes.

Someone said: "What other people think of me is none of my business!" As Taylor Swift says, "What I do with my life is nobody's business." But if *you* ever want to share, your precious secrets will be safe with me.

Look how we can offer others what we still can't grant ourselves.

About the Author
Anonymous

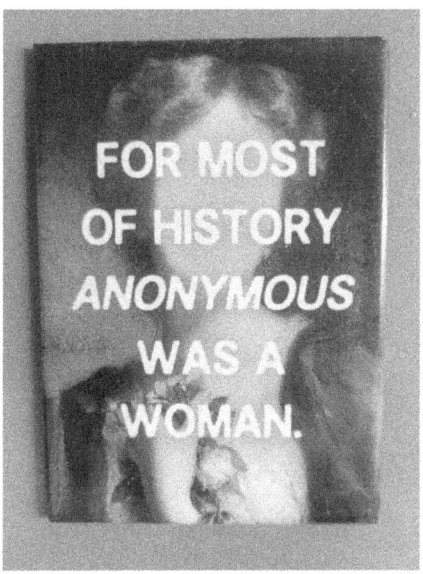

The decision to remain anonymous is one of profound complexity. For many, especially women, sharing a story under their own name comes with risks—of judgment, misunderstanding, and even retribution. It is a choice made not out of shame, but out of necessity, reflecting the societal pressures and stigmas that still silence so many voices.

For centuries, women have carried their stories in silence, fearing the consequences of speaking their truths. Fear of alienation from loved ones, damage to professional reputations, or rejection by communities often forces these narratives into the shadows. Yet, these stories matter. They are the unspoken threads that weave our collective human experience, full of pain, hope, and resilience.

This anonymous author speaks for those who cannot. By choosing to shield their identity, they protect themselves and others while still contributing to the vital dialogue that *Taboo: Stories That Can't Be Told* seeks to foster. Their words remind us that courage takes many forms, and that every story shared—named or nameless—is a step toward breaking the chains of silence.

May this author's voice resonate with those who have yet to find the freedom to share their own truths. Silence may be forced upon some, but the power of the story endures.

Thank you

Dear Reader,

    If you have enjoyed or found value in this book, please take a moment to leave an honest/brief review on Amazon amzn.to/4fUUrx2 or Goodreads. Your reviews help prospective readers decide if this is right for them & it is the greatest kindness you can offer the authors.

    Thank you in advance.

Acknowledgments

This book is the result of countless moments from mentors, teacher and guides. It is the culmination of our own dreams and the learning from our own struggles. It is in this process of writing that we both share our vulnerable selves and offer a gift forth for the readers.

Through the bravery of its authors and the support of the team we share this act of love.

In particular our author mentors that supported writers:

- Erika Hull
- Mimi Rich

These women have shared, coached and guided the contributors through the technical, logistical and emotional journey that is writing and becoming an author.

Thanks to all who have led us to this moment. May it ripple.

Other Red Thread Books

Our books about writing & publishing:

The Anatomy of a Book: 21 Book Experts Share What Aspiring Authors Need to Know About Writing, Publishing & Book Marketing

Typo: The Art of Imperfect Creation, *Permission to Do it Badly*

Story Ink: *A Cyclical Methodology to Write 1 or 100 books* (2024)

Write: *An Interactive Guide to Drafting Your Manuscript* (forthcoming)

To see all our published works Visit Our Library:

bit.ly/RedThreadLibrary

Previous Collaborative Titles in the Brave New Voices Series:

Feisty: *Dangerously Amazing Women Using Their Voices & Making An Impact*

Spark: *Women in the Business of Changing the World*

Sanctuary: *Cultivating Safe Space in Sisterhood; Rediscovering the Power that Unites Us*

Sisterhood Redefines Us (Collaborative)
We are stronger together, but we must find or create our own safety first. (10 authors)

Dangerously Amazing Women (Collaborative)
If you're ready to rewrite all the rules & start thriving, just as you are, then Feisty is a must-read! (19 authors)

Women In the Business of Changing the World (Collaborative)
Celebrating the extraordinary impact of ordinary women, when we show up & shine in our full, unapologetic authority. (10 authors)

Planting the Seed: *Lessons to Cultivate a Brighter Future*
Notes From Motherland: *The Wild Adventure of Raising Humans*
By the Light of the Moon

Write & Publish with Us as a Collaborative Author

Be the next **Red Thread Collaborative Author**: bit.ly/46Yd6Ed

Why write with us

Our collaborative authors get full support in the drafting, editing and publishing process. We teach all our authors about book marketing & authorprenur essentials. We work as a collective and have a wider reach and more impact as a result.

If a book is like a baby, writing in a collaborative is like being an auntie; all the joy with a fraction of the effort of writing and publishing an entire book yourself.

*All royalties from this book fund our Author Scholarship Program. We believe in powerful stories and support otherwise silenced voices to be heard.

Access our Free Author Resources

bit.ly/RedThreadResources

Red Thread Publishing

We are a dynamic publishing company that produces high-quality, nonfiction books that inspire, educate, and entertain our readers. Our small team is passionate about literature and committed to supporting authors in sharing their stories with the world. We are celebrating our third year & our 60th book published!

Red Thread Publishing houses two imprints. **Red Thread Books** was founded to support 10,000 **women** to become successful published authorpreneurs & thought leaders. We have expanded to incorporate a second imprint **Red Falcon Press** for all genders, encouraging more silenced and marginalized folks to share their voices & stories.

To date, we have supported 290 people from 30 countries to Write & Publish their books. To work with us or connect regarding any of our growing library of books email us at **info@redthreadbooks.com**. To learn more about us visit our website **www.redthreadbooks.com**.

Follow us & join the community.

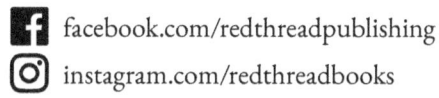

facebook.com/redthreadpublishing

instagram.com/redthreadbooks

www.ingramcontent.com/pod-product-compliance
Lightning Source LLC
Chambersburg PA
CBHW020547030426
42337CB00013B/991